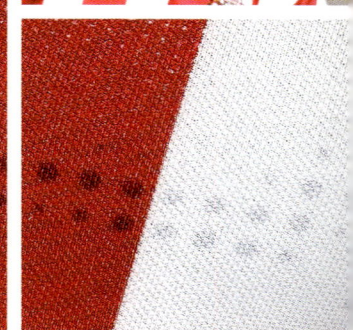

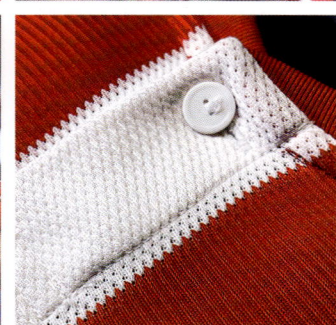

KIT CATS SAFC'S STADIUM OF LIGHT KIT STORY
WRITTEN BY ANDREW SMITHSON & ROB MASON

A TWOCAN PUBLICATION

©2021. Published by twocan under licence from Sunderland AFC.

ISBN: 978-1-913362-92-8

PICTURE CREDITS: Action Images, Alamy, Oscar Chamberlain, Ian Horrocks, Brian Leng, Rob Mason, Sunderland AFC.

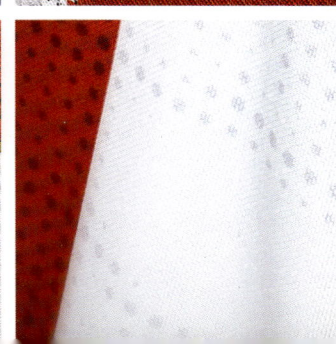

KIT CATTS

FOREWORD BY LEE CATTERMOLE

Having spent ten seasons at Sunderland and played over 250 games, I have to say I thoroughly enjoyed my time at the Stadium of Light. As you would expect at any club we had our highs and lows, but eight of those years were in the Premier League and we reached Wembley three times.

2015-16

2014-15

2016-17

We had many managers / head coaches, playing styles and playing kits. Every manager or head coach brings his own philosophy and you try to learn from all of them. I particularly learned from Gus Poyet.

We played some terrific football under him, forged a clear identity on the pitch and after knocking Chelsea and Manchester United out of the competition, gave a really good account of ourselves in the Capital One Cup final against Manchester City in 2014, when only a couple of absolute worldies turned a game we were deservedly leading in.

The run in to the end of that season where we won away to Chelsea and Manchester United in the Premier League, and were only denied a win at City through a late equaliser, was one of several times where we fought to the last to stay up. We would rather have not been involved in such battles, but mostly we won them and did so with spirit, and at times in some style.

When it comes to the kits, Sunderland's red and white stripes are known throughout the game. Everywhere we played, whether it was home or away, you could always count on there being huge support with fans proudly sporting their stripes. Sunderland possess massive support and so many of the people who follow the club want to show that support by sporting the kit themselves. The release of the new home and away kits always excites people as it means the new season is just around the corner and everyone has their own favourite strips.

2017-18

2013-14

For me, my favourite would be the 2014-15 kit, and I particularly liked the one-off kit that we wore under the lights that season at Palace for an away win live on Sky, but what matters most is what is inside the strip. Players should have pride in the shirt because ultimately you have to want to do well for the people you are playing for and you have to have professional pride in yourself. I tried to do that in every single one of the 261 games I played for Sunderland and I'm proud to have done so for so long.

In Lee Cattermole's decade at Sunderland he played alongside 144 teammates, more than any other player in the club's entire history. As well as being an inspirational captain Lee also became only the sixth player, and the first this century, to score in three different divisions for the club.

INTRODUCTION

Sunderland are synonymous with red and white stripes, even if the club's original colours were blue. For most of the pre-Stadium of Light era, football kits did not change often, but in recent decades it has become expected that clubs will reveal new kits on an annual basis and many supporters eagerly anticipate the latest designs.

Kit Cats looks at the kits of the Black Cats. Each home and away outfit since the Stadium of Light opened is focussed on, including the strips worn by the goalkeepers. There is also an extensive feature on every kit worn by SAFC at Wembley as well as the strip worn in the club's first FA Cup final (or English Cup as it was more commonly known then) in 1913, before Wembley was built.

We hope that Sunderland supporters enjoy re-living their favourite, and perhaps not so favourite, strips. In particular in the 'Rare cat sightings' section, we hope you also find some kits you have forgotten Sunderland ever played in, if you ever knew in the first place! Hands up everyone who remembers Sunderland playing in orange!

'Kit Story' examines the development of the team's playing kit from the days when blue was the colour to the time when red and white was introduced, but in halves not stripes. Continuing through the three different centuries red and white stripes have been worn, the development and variations of those stripes - and indeed the shorts and socks - have been closely examined.

A full Stadium of Light includes tens of thousands of supporters wearing Sunderland strips of all variations. In Kit Cats you can explore the many kits the lads have worn. If you have a break, enjoy Kit Cats.

1913 FA CUP FINAL SHIRT

THE ORANGE SHIRT FROM 1986-87

PAPA JOHN'S TROPHY WINNERS 2021

ACKNOWLEDGEMENTS

The authors would like to thank Paul Briggs and twocan design for backing this project. We would also like to thank Lindsay Douglas and Alex Middleton of Sunderland AFC for their interest and support.

Thanks are also due to Ronnie Scott, kit collector Kevan Ball for the loan of several of the rare tops seen in this book, including the all red shirt seen on page 139, and 'Spaceturtle' of the Ready to Go site.

'Sunderland: The Absolute Record' co-author Barry Jackson has also been of great assistance in providing copies of old Football Echo's verifying descriptions of several of Sunderland's kit changes. Mike Gibson who also co-authored, 'Sunderland: The Absolute Record' with Rob Mason has also been an invaluable help as always.

3

III 2021 22

The home shirt for the 25th season at the Stadium of Light is one of the most bespoke the club has had this century.

SAFC's Graphic Designer, Alex Middleton and Head of Retail, Lindsay Douglas had the unique opportunity to work on the design for 2021-22 alongside Nike. Having worked at SAFC for over thirty years between them, they are understandably proud to have been involved in the process. "It's an honour to be part of such a prestigious project, in terms of things we've done at Sunderland, we can't top this" said Middleton.

"The shirt is a kind of hybrid of design elements from three historical shirts. The largely white base on the '83 to '86 Nike home, the faded stripes on the '95 to '97 Avec away, and the subtle crest on the 09-10 Umbro home." The latter can be credited for inspiring the large abstract crest which adorns the front of the garment, "We like those discovery elements: you definitely won't see it on TV, but when you're six feet away you're going to look at that detail and appreciate it. The challenge was to create something different, evidentially bespoke to us, whilst being respectful to a traditional Sunderland shirt and hopefully we have managed to achieve that." The shirt also sees Great Annual Savings continue their invaluable support and sponsorship of the club into 2021-22.

As any kit is being developed it is kept closely under wraps until it is ready for release. Internally once the initial design had progressed the idea was put to Director of Football Kristjaan Speakman and Chief Operating Officer Steve Davison who gave their approval as the project gathered pace.

AIDEN McGEADY SCORED THE FIRST GOALS IN THE 2021-22 KIT WITH A BRACE IN A PRE-SEASON WIN AT HEARTS

USA INTERNATIONAL LYNDEN GOOCH IS ALWAYS A STAR IN STRIPES

Sunderland's strip for 2021-22 is not radically different to what has gone before, but ultimately of course the popularity of a strip and how it is remembered is inextricably linked with how well the team does. Hopefully in years to come the 2021-22 kit will be remembered as the kit of a promotion winning year.

The striking yellow and blue away strip could also end up being viewed as a classic in future years after a positive initial response, with the round neck shirt featuring the same Nike zig zag detailing that was worn by England's outfield players in the UEFA EURO 2020 final ten days prior to its release and a pattern on the raglan sleeves that matched the one seen on Jordan Pickford during the tournament.

It was unveiled with the help of local band ZELA, who modelled the shirt at the Eppleton Colliery Welfare Ground used by the club for some U23s and Ladies games, following on from the 'Remix' theme of the home kit that reflected the nod to previous strips and saw DJ and Sunderland fan Sorley mark its release at the Academy of Light with a reworked version of Dance of the Knights. The goalkeepers meanwhile had a remix of their own, with the same design as last season being reissued but in different colourways - the primary choices being all black or royal blue.

Having already seen Sunderland's kits for 2021-22 the remainder of Kit Cats tells the story of the Sunderland strip. Focussing on every home and away outfit from the Stadium of Light era, this is followed by features on every SAFC Cup final and Wembley kit and an examination of some kits worn so rarely that in some cases they were only worn once.

CALLUM DOYLE IN RED AND WHITE FOR THE FIRST TIME AT HEARTS HAVING JOINED ON LOAN FROM MANCHESTER CITY

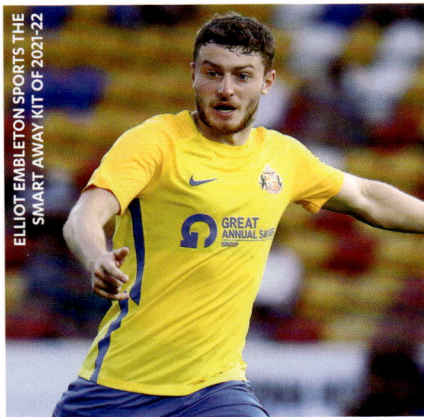

ELLIOT EMBLETON SPORTS THE SMART AWAY KIT OF 2021-22

REPUBLIC OF IRELAND INTERNATIONAL AIDEN O'BRIEN

KIT STORY

SUNDERLAND AFC GOES HAND IN HAND WITH RED AND WHITE STRIPES

The colours permeate several aspects of the club, and throughout the Stadium of Light era are even referenced in the title of the match day programmes.

JOHNNY CAMPBELL 1891-92

BOBBY KERR 1966-67

NIALL QUINN 1996-97

THE FIRST DAY THE LADS WORE RED & WHITE STRIPES SATURDAY 24 SEPTEMBER 1887

This was not the case during the clubs formulative days however, and in their early games, the team wore an all blue kit believed to have been selected due to the fact Sunderland's first home ground was The Blue House Field. It was in 1884 when the club switched to red and white, and even then, it was in the form of halve shirts at first.

With the white sections placed on the left hand side (right hand side as you look), and the sleeve colours alternating from the main torso pieces, these tops featured stub collars. A squad photo from 1885-86 shows that captain James McMillan and Nicholas Hornsby both had shirts that included chest pockets with what look like the initials 'SFC' embroidered on them, but the only other emblems were those awarded to players with representative honours, namely for County Durham. By the start of 1886-87, the shirts had changed again with the halves being flipped so that the left hand side was now red, albeit with white chest pockets, and the sleeve arrangement was altered so that the fronts now matched the side of the shirt they were on.

This kit was retained for the start of the 1887-88 season, although shortly into the campaign came the first appearance of the stripes that are now so synonymous with Sunderland. Manufacturing techniques had improved so that such shirts were now easier to produce and so on the 24th of September 1887, the team took to the field for their game against St. Augustine's (from Darlington) in red and white stripes, albeit with white 'knickerbockers'. Goalkeeper Bill Kirtley meanwhile still wore a halved shirt.

Many players wore belts with their knickerbockers and at this point, it was common for sides to regularly change the colour of these, although photographs from the time suggest Sunderland moved to black in time for the following season. The main facets now arrived upon; Sunderland's kit continued to evolve over the coming years as fashions changed, with first the collar type and pattern being altered, and the stripes themselves becoming broader.

In 1890, Sunderland's second ever game in the Football League prompted a major change in kit protocol. Visitors Wolverhampton Wanderers also wore red and white stripes, and as a result, teams had to register their colours going forwards with sides not allowed to select the same ones. When Division Two was formed, the rules were relaxed and clubs were instead instructed to keep a set of white shirts, although it was usually the home team that would be required to use these 'change' kits, as is known to have been the case during the opening game of Sunderland's 1901-02 title-winning season when they entertained Sheffield United.

When Sunderland legend Ted Doig was at the club, it was common for goalkeepers to wear the same strips as the rest of the team, although in Doig's case, the decision to wear a cap in addition might have been more to do with vanity than practicality, and distinguishing himself from the outfield players - the Scot being famously conscious of his hair, or more accurately the lack of it. The buttons of the shirts would sometimes continue as far down as the naval, although in 1904, the same year Doig moved on, the club introduced a new design with laced collars.

This style remained for several years, although the socks, whilst dark in the main, were regularly tweaked slightly and featured different turnover designs. It was not until 1909 that stoppers were instructed to wear different tops to the rest of their teammates, and twelve years later the Football

SUNDERLAND AFC IN RED & WHITE HALVED SHIRTS 1886-87

2ND DIVISION CHAMPIONS

1975/6

1976-77

LE COQ SPORTIF'S INFAMOUS 'CANDY STRIPE' SHIRT, 1981-83

League stipulated that it should now be the visiting side that should change kit in the instance of a colour clash. This was not the case in the FA Cup however for several decades, and at some points both sides would be required to change strips in cup ties.

During the 1930s, Sunderland changed back to buttoned collars again. Photographs from the period suggested that some players had started removing the laces from their collars prior to this anyway, presumably for comfort, and short sleeves were introduced now too, so that they did not have to keep rolling them up.

In May 1933, Sunderland travelled to France and ticked off a couple of 'firsts' against Racing Club de Paris, with the match being played under floodlights and the players wearing numbers on their backs. It was not until the end of the decade that numbers became mandatory in the league, although the years in between Sunderland had once more been crowned champions of England, and in 2021 remain the last club wearing stripes to have done so.

These were halcyon days in Sunderland's history. They followed up their 1935-36 league title by winning the FA Cup in 1937, but just as impressive as the players were their kits, which must have been almost indestructible as they were seen still being used in one squad photograph taken over a decade later.

Of course, early photographs still being in black and white and the scarcity of footage make tracking all of Sunderland's early kits very difficult. The photos that are available, confirm that the team still sometimes used white shirts and black shorts as an alternative strip in the late 1940s, when the most noticeable change to the home kit was the introduction of hooped socks. Before that, black socks with red turnovers had been prominent for over twenty years, save for a period during World War II when Sunderland used red with white turnovers.

The following decade saw a big shift in style as the 'continental' look became widespread as new lightweight materials and less bulky cuts were introduced. The red socks with white turnovers became a long-term feature and in 1955, the Lads started using shirts with white deep v-neck collars, although these were then replaced with a more discreet red v-neck in later seasons.

The centre stripe started as red, but even in the same game players would sometimes wear slightly different shirts to one another and be seen with a white stripe central instead. Goalkeepers also bought into the changes, with the thicker or ribbed 'ganseys' perhaps more associated with Sunderland comedian Bobby Thompson now making way.

Thompson was a popular act, but Sunderland remained the big draw for crowds whether home or away, where white shirts often continued to be used, although now they sometimes had red collars. They would sometimes be paired with white shorts also, mirroring those used with the home kit from 1961 onwards, a change that was instigated by manager Alan Brown and was first seen during a 2-1 home win against Stoke City in August. The shorts remained for over a decade, but despite that successful debut they were never fully accepted by supporters.

There was a further modification when red socks were incorporated into the home strip in 1964, by which point Sunderland were also using a sky blue shirt in some away games with either matching or darker shorts. Things continued to move with the times and in 1965 the traditional red and white shirt was updated again and now featured a crew collar.

Standards were not exact however, and the players continued to take to the pitch in a mixture of shirts that featured different coloured central stripes, or perhaps more jarringly, no central stripe at all. This period also saw the team wearing new change kits, with all red and all white options being utilised.

In some instances, these shirts were embroidered with the initials 'SAFC', whilst there were additional trim details on the shorts used in some fixtures, but there were not any hard and fast rules to this and these features seemed to come and go at various points. Black shorts also made an appearance on some trips, and in 1969, the Football League moved once more to formalise the use of change kits and started instructing visiting clubs to change their shorts or socks if they were too similar to their hosts', even if they did not clash directly.

The reintroduction of white turnovers for the 1969-70 season were not enough to stave off relegation, but the 1970s saw further developments in kit design and more acutely, the marketing of them. As manufacturers looked to trademark their products and sell official replicas to supporters, mainly younger ones at this point, shirts were no longer seen as generic or ad hoc items of sporting equipment and several clubs introduced new images that they hoped would capture the public's imagination.

Sunderland, thankfully, did not try anything too gaudy, but whilst their home strips remained fairly standard, the Lads did have a flurry of different change kits. Contemporary sources such as match day programmes or the Football Echo did not always feature images from away days and TV cameras were still a long way away from becoming ubiquitous at football grounds, but in August, September and October 1970 alone, the side are known to have worn three different away kits - with a sky blue outfit now being used in addition to the existing white and red options.

Those strips were all quite plain. After winning the FA Cup in 1973, Sunderland's kits began showing more elements of design however, with makers Umbro including their logo, their iconic club initials feature and the inscription 'FA Cup Winners 1973' on the following season's home strips. In 1975, a new button collar was introduced on a shirt with serrated stripe edges and whilst this kit proudly boasted the words '2nd Division Champions 1975-76' during the following season, Sunderland actually wore their 1973-74 strip again during the victory over Portsmouth that secured the title. Anybody that has seen footage or images from the subsequent trophy presentation may notice that the players are then wearing the properly designated kit again, but that is because this took place two days later during Bobby Kerr's testimonial.

Changing tack was not uncommon to Sunderland. Bob Stokoe's immediate decision following his arrival as manager in November 1972 to revert to using black shorts with the home strip proved to be an instant hit with the majority of fans, and then having used a striking yellow away kit at the start of 1976-77, it had been altered by the autumn to include a blue collar that matched the trimming.

That kit was combined with black shorts for some instances and had replaced white as Sunderland's 'go-to' alternative, with the club having primarily used designs with a red collar and red and black trim, and then a basic white shirt with matching collar, since winning the FA Cup.

Both these tops included the club initials, as it was still uncommon for clubs to wear their official crests at this point, and it was only from 1977-78 onwards that Sunderland's shirts began to bear the famous ship badge, despite it having first been released five years earlier.

During the late 1960s and early 1970s, Sunderland had two distinct club crests, one an uncomplicated shield with three stripes and 'Sunderland AFC' running along the top, which was then tweaked slightly and subsequently read simply 'SAFC', and the other a more complex design that featured in the middle a black cat sat on top of a football. Neither of these were seen on kits, but did feature elsewhere, such as on letterheads, in copies of the Roker Review and on other club issue clothing.

When the 'new' badge, still familiar to many fans even now, was then introduced onto the kits, it helped complete what is still arguably the quintessential Sunderland look - the open collar design was used for four seasons, although in 1980-81, it was reworked slightly to make use of newer man-made fabrics, had a new number font and the badge was repositioned slightly.

During this period, Sunderland rotated between different kits at away games. The yellow choice was used until at least 1979, at which point, a sharp white design was introduced. A royal blue look that spanned the other two kits was also in use and is of course best remembered for being worn when Gary Rowell scored a hat-trick against Newcastle United in that same year.

The shirt featured a very 70s looking wide collar with red and white detailing that matched that of the cuffs, plus braiding down the sleeves that was similar to that of the yellow kit it was first used in conjunction with, although this braid was amended slightly on later incarnations. It was combined with red, white, and even black shorts on occasion, depending on the opposition, whilst the white version was also seen with both white and black shorts and had similar trim that was instead, blue and red. This kit was also used for another famous victory on Tyneside when the Lads beat Newcastle on penalties in the 1979-80 League Cup, and then again two months later when the club won the Daily Express Five-a-Side Championships at Wembley Arena.

Whilst Sunderland's previous kits had been somewhat iconic, when new manufacturers came on board in 1981, they ripped up the rule book and released a kit like nothing else seen before by the Rokerites. Whereas in the 1940s and 50s, man-mountains like Fred Hall would fill the shirts with muscle, Sunderland's uncluttered stripes after that made even the strongest of players look lean and lithe. Kit suppliers were getting more adventurous all the time though, and with the new fit not exactly leaving much to the imagination, the narrow stripes, or 'candy stripes' as many supporters knew them as, brought out by French firm Le Coq Sportif were even more slimming.

For some, that was about as much as could be said for the shirts, which were more than just experimental and did not go down well with the majority of supporters. The kit featured an element of black in the design, Sunderland's traditional colours having long since been red, white and black of course, but this was the first time black had been seen on the shirt as part of the actual pattern, and whilst it has featured on them periodically ever since, few of the other touches lasted as long.

The shorts too were a massive shift from the norm, and like the accompanying socks were bright red - a point not lost on those who felt the shirt did not have nearly enough of the colour. Even now, the kit raises the hackles of some when brought up in conversation, but interestingly, recent reproductions of the shirt are seen regularly in the stands on matchdays.

The corresponding away kit is another retro favourite now, although even at the time, this did seem to strike more of a chord with fans. That might be simply because it was being compared to the home version, but they shared many design features such as v-neck collars, the maker's logos being on the sleeves and the club badge being placed over the middle of the chest. A light blue shirt with darker pin stripes, it was usually paired with corresponding shorts and socks, although the home shorts did have to be worn with it still in certain matches.

After two years with those strips, Sunderland became the first European club to wear kits provided by Nike, who have since gone on to be a major force in the market and still have premises in the city. At the time, the multi-national company had a base in Coniston House in Washington, and in addition to the home kit, which reintroduced traditional black shorts, but retained the all red socks, Nike supplied a change kit and a third kit. All three strips were from very similar templates, with the away version once more being a light blue with darker horizontal stripes and sleeves, and the additional kit a yellow design with dark trim.

Aficionados often note that the club crests and makers logos were on the 'wrong side' of these shirts, and anecdotal evidence suggests that the badges were placed in an unfamiliar location on the right hand side of the shirts because they were from existing training-wear stock which had the maker's logo already on it. It was certainly the case that if you bought a replica, the crest would be separate and still needed to be individually sewn on with a needle and thread, but Nike were the first company to also include a badge on Sunderland's shorts, and whilst the subsequent supplier did not follow suit, this is now a staple feature on almost all major clubs' kits.

The other main point related to these Nike kits is that they featured sponsor logos for the first time in Sunderland's history. Other clubs had already started dabbling in this area, but had been forced to revert to their plain kits when featuring on television - these rules were then relaxed however, and with Sunderland's home game against Manchester United in October 1983 due to be featured on Match of the Day, owner Tom Cowie OBE (he was not knighted until nine years later) included the name of his motor vehicle and transport empire on the shirts.

As it was, the programme did not air due to industrial disputes at the BBC and despite getting off to an inauspicious start with a defeat to the Red Devils, sponsorship was here to stay and soon became a constant feature on Sunderland's strips. As the regulations altered further, the Cowies logo changed size and font a couple of times, and since then, several major firms have adorned the kits.

Supporters will often take an element of pride in bearing the logo of a popular local employer, and several renowned national and international firms have also featured on shirts over the years - as well as the main first-team sponsorship deals, both the Co-Op (North Eastern) and Tudor Crips were seen on the kits used by some of the club's youth and community sides in the early days of sponsorship, and as recently as 2019, Sunderland AFC Ladies had a tie-in that saw them displaying the logo of Wash & Go during games.

When Sunderland were relegated from Division One in 1985, the Nike kits were retained, with a mocked-up version of the home shirt used on the front cover of the following season's match day programmes that actually displayed the club crest on the 'correct' side.

Early editions showed an embroidered badge, but this was soon replaced with a graphic that also featured the logo of Vaux, who had just begun what would become a long standing commercial deal between two famous Sunderland institutions.

During their time as main club sponsor, the brewery elected at different points to display on the tops either their own name or that of some of their individual beers. Samson, Scorpion Lager, Lambton's and Tuborg, which at the time it was seen, between 1985 and 1988, was brewed under license at the plant, all featured. Sometimes these logos would appear as a separate patch sewn onto the player issue kits, whilst replicas would have them placed directly on the shirt.

Goalkeepers, not just at Sunderland but elsewhere too, would not always wear the shirts that were issued by their club's main provider. The first designs handed to Sunderland by both Le Coq Sportif and Nike were similar in appearance to the ones being worn during most of the 1970s and early 1980s, and whilst both firms then replaced these with more contemporary efforts, they were not always seen in first-team matches.

This was particularly noticeable during the 1985-86 campaign, when Sunderland struggled to find a permanent number one and the shirt itself changed a couple of times too. Stoppers had begun getting their own glove or boot deals and were wearing tops provided by more specialist goalkeeping firms, with Bob Bolder and Andy Dibble usually wearing an Uhlsport shirt, and Seamus McDonagh a jersey-like sweater, neither of which featured the club badge, but did still bear sponsor logos.

Goalkeepers going against the grain is nothing new in football, but such individualism might seem unfathomable now. At this point, club-specific replica goalie shirts were not widely available, but with these strips since proving popular with fans and collectors, clubs and suppliers alike prefer their players to be wearing the correctly assigned gear.

After Nike, the next company to make strips for Sunderland were Patrick, who worked with the club for two years up until 1988 and oddly enough, gave over goalkeeper strips that were almost identical to the Uhlsport tops worn previously, in terms of collar and sleeve designs and again did not always feature the club badge.

When it was seen, the badge was placed in the centre of the chest area like it was on the v-neck outfield strips, which all shared the same detailing on the collars and cuffs and bore Patrick logos on the sleeves. The away tops featured shadow stripes and were light blue once more, but whereas the previous home kit had featured solid white sleeves, they were now red. The biggest alteration to Sunderland's look however, was the introduction of all white socks, although alternate red shorts once again had to be utilised on occasions, and white shorts were sometimes paired with both kits.

The 80s and 90s were a tumultuous time in Sunderland's history, even by its own standards. The 1988-89 campaign brought a rare mid-table finish, but it was also the first time that the club wore kits made by Danish brand Hummel, whose British arm was operating out of Enfield and was working with several other high profile teams at the time.

In a decade that had seen all sorts of departures from their characteristic home look, Hummel brought out a design that, whilst still keeping up with the times, was more in keeping with Sunderland's traditions.

The first batch of home kits stated 'Third Division Champions 87-88' above the club badge and the following season, supporters could buy a version which read 'Centenary Year 1989-1990, 100 years in the Football League', but replica shirts during the Hummel era differed from player issue ones as instead of being embroidered, the badges were an embossed foam-like material. There was a further addition to the kits from 1990-91, when players started wearing small Football League sleeve patches that remained on Sunderland's shirts until the middle of the decade.

The first away kit to be provided by Hummel was a much darker shade of blue than had been seen in other recent change strips, but it was the goalkeepers that saw the most notable advancement in Sunderland kit culture; after first wearing a design with trademark chevrons and diagonal lines along the top half of the torso, a new design was introduced part way through the 1989-90 season and the green version became the first to be sold in volume to supporters.

There was also a slate blue alternative that was not available for retail, with both options using the same pattern template and black shoulder and lower arm patches. At different points, the sponsoring on player issue versions switched between black and white fonts, but the design was retained when new outfield kits were brought out for the 1991-92 season, albeit there was a slight change to reflect the fact Sunderland had tweaked their club badge. This was not the first time the ship crest had been rebranded; several alternative versions have been used by the club at different points, but in terms of the ones seen on the kits, the design first seen from 1977 had been toned down a decade earlier and now saw the colouring changed again.

This slimmed down version of the crest was just one new feature of what proved to be two very popular outfield kits, with the away strip often cited as an all-time favourite by some supporters. Certainly the kits are associated with a positive period in the history of Sunderland as a place; on 14 February 1992, it was granted City Status by Queen Elizabeth II (whose mother had presented the FA Cup to the Lads in 1937) and when a 'City Celebration Match' was staged at Roker in August of that year against Tottenham Hotspur, they were depicted on the front cover of the match day programme. Future editions that season also included the home kit graphic on the front, but alongside the shirt of the visiting team instead.

When the Lads made the short trip to Middlesbrough in October 1993, the backs of their shirts featured player names and squad numbers for the first time, and apart from three seasons later in the decade, these have been present ever since. The match also saw Sunderland turn out in their brand new yellow and black third kit for the first time, but this was to be the last strip supplied by Hummel as from 1994-95 onwards, Avec took over.

The first British firm to supply Sunderland's kits since Umbro, Avec were even closer to home as they were a subsidiary of County Durham company Claremont Garments, and their gear was first worn for a disappointing home defeat to Oxford United in April 1994. There was little riding on the game, this season seeing the only other mid-table finish of the era, but Sunderland were about to undergo a massive change and so the firm were part of the club's first foray into the Premiership and their final days at Roker Park.

Avec had a hard act to follow. The previous two sets of kits were much loved, but in an era where all manner of outlandish designs were being seen

THE BLUE CHANGE KIT FROM 1986-88

DON GOODMAN 1993

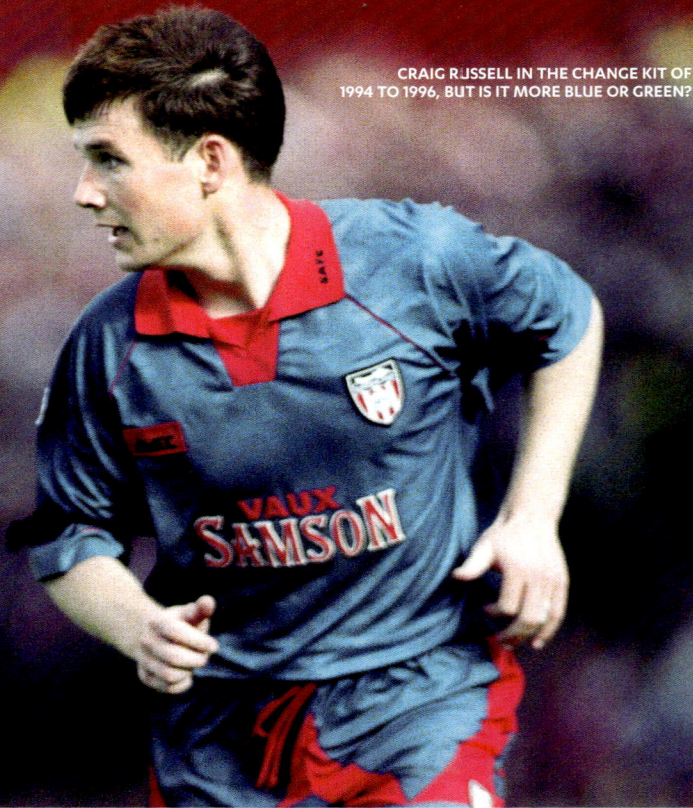

elsewhere, Sunderland's outfield players got off relatively lightly with contemporary, yet well-liked strips. The home shirt did feature some artistic license, with a large red panel near one shoulder and a stray line running towards the other, but the traditional Sunderland look was still there in essence.

Displaying the Vaux Samson logo, this kit was soon being worn proudly by Sunderland's new mascot - whose name was taken from the beer. Samson the Cat, who was later brought to life on matchdays by future Managing Director Tony Davison, was subsequently joined by Delilah and to go with the black cats, the cuffs on the home tops were also black. The shirts also featured the initials 'SAFC' on the collar, with the same polo neck design being used for the away kit.

Advertised as 'teal', this strip prompted many school yard and bar room debates about whether it leaned towards being blue or green. Finished with red trim, both this strip and the home one saw the club badge included on the socks again and came with shorts that had additional flourishes. It was the goalkeepers however, that really bore the brunt of the craze for heavily patterned kit, being given a top so loud it was off the scale - no the wonder that when asked for his thoughts on it, Tony Norman replied simply with, "Can I have a plain green one?"

Despite the brashness, the mosaic design that featured the outline of a pair of goalkeeping gloves, is now a bit of a cult classic. This was the first time the stoppers were given bespoke shorts, and with the following design seeing bespoke socks introduced also, the move towards goalkeepers having a fully separate identity was complete.

With the goalkeeper's kit being described as 'alternative', the outfield players did still have to use different combinations in some instances. In March 1995, the Lads picked up back-to-back away wins at Watford and Southend United whilst wearing red shorts, and eleven months later, the team used basic white socks at Portsmouth in a 2-2 draw. The next nine games were all won, and although the Lads could only draw at Watford in the tenth game, when this time they had white shorts, the run helped them secure the Division One title.

During the promotion season, Sunderland's preferred change kit was a yellow and teal design that had initially been released towards the end of 1994-95, when it was originally advertised as a third kit. Again, featuring the club crest on the socks like that season's other kits, and sharing the same micro-pattern detailing of the outfield strips that featured the manufacturer's stylised 'A' logo, it was different in that the shirt and short crests were now on a shield background, and the tops had a new collar design with large lapels.

Although designed to be worn extremely baggy again, during this period the idea of football shirts being part of a supporter's day to day identity started to really ramp up. Club branded leisure wear also became much more common place, and with the days of former players such as Charlie Buchan and Willie Watson owning sports shops long gone, Sunderland ran several official club shops and concessions across the region.

As well as the Shop on the Park at Roker and then later the Stadium Store, the club has had multiple outlets in the centre of Sunderland and places like Washington, Durham and Bishop Auckland.

The much-loved Roker Rover double decker bus would also undertake tours of the region at Christmas time during parts of the 1990s so that supporters could buy club merchandise, and whilst some areas of Tyneside may not been seen as Sunderland heartlands by one or two people, many will point to the fact these were traditionally part of County Durham and that the strong level of support coming from there more than justified the opening of units in South Shields and the Metrocentre in Gateshead. There was even a stall at Newcastle International Airport in more recent times, with the club looking to capitalise on the thirst for English football from foreign visitors to the north east.

Winning Division One meant that 1996-97, Sunderland's final campaign in SR6, would be in the top flight, but when manager Peter Reid exclaimed that the players would be 'happy to be seen in the discotheque' wearing the Farewell to Roker kits, he was perhaps pointing more towards the close team sprit he had helped foster, than the growing trend of football shirts being seen as a fashion item in their own right. The strips looked smart either way though, and whilst they harked back to simpler styles, there were still one or two modern twists such as small tags on the sides that read 'Roker Park 1898-1997'.

Both outfield kits had red v-neck collars and cuffs, and labels by the hem that read 'Authentic Product from Sunderland AFC 99 Years at Roker Park Supplied by Avec Sportswear', with those buying a replica version being given a commemorative certificate of authenticity. The home strip, which was worn for the final home game of the previous season and the ensuing trophy presentation, saw the reintroduction of hooped socks and within the red stripes of the shirts, micro-patterned detailing that listed the four different stands at Roker Park. The white stripes, and the white away top, featured repeated copies of the maker's logo and the words '1898-1997 Roker Park'.

With the change shorts being white, they were sometimes used alongside the home top for some away games, and in some others, the change shirt was instead paired with the black shorts primarily meant for the home kit. Sunderland still used the yellow and teal kit on occasions too.

On the new kits, the club crests, which Avec had again embroidered on the shirts, now sat upon larger shields that also read 'Roker Park 1898-1997.' They were placed on the middle of the chest area on the goalkeeper kits, which were made from a quilted-like material and were heavily padded. The home version of the design was green and change version was yellow, with both incorporating black detailing.

These were the last strips worn by the Lads during the Roker Park era, with the visit of Liverpool bringing about the end of nearly a century of football history. There was an element of symmetry about the match, the visitors had provided the opposition for the ground's inaugural game and on both occasions it finished 1-0 to the hosts, but this time it was the guests that were wearing white shirts with dark shorts, when 99 years earlier it had been Sunderland wearing those change colours. Kits have indeed evolved immeasurably since then, and the idea of the Lads playing at home in anything but red and white now seems almost alien.

Following the move from Roker, 'pit gear' took on a new meaning as the site of the former Wearmouth Colliery was transformed into the Stadium of Light, and pit boots were replaced by football boots, hard hats were replaced by bobble hats, black dust was replaced by Black Cats and coal by goals.

Donkey jackets might still make an appearance in the stands on cold evenings admittedly, but the uniform for the majority filing in and out now would be red and white in the main.

Since then, over 300 different players have pulled on a shirt, whilst thousands more have instead bought one and dreamt of the doing the same. One player that matched the supporters in terms of determination to see the club succeed was Lee Cattermole, who has kindly provided the foreword for this book and who many will remember could be very particular in how he tucked his shirt in. That pride in the shirt is what fans demand, and they expect to see players giving their all for the badge.

The current crest was introduced as part of the complete overhaul the club underwent when moving to the stadium that was overseen by the now titled Sir Bob Murray CBE. Since then, Sunderland have worn many kits, and whilst the styles, fits and materials have all developed over time, the badge has remained virtually the same throughout, other than in 2016-17 when on the third kit, a stylised monochrome version was used.

That strip was a pink and purple design, but the campaign was anything but pretty in pink and Sunderland were relegated from the Premier League. Despite the negative connotations however, the shirt is harder to come by than most other replicas from that period and when they do become available via online auction sites or through traders, collectors have to pay a slight premium.

As well as replicas, match-worn shirts are also highly sought after items, particularly so from the period where the kit bag would contain just a couple of spare, unnumbered 'blood' shirts to be used in case of emergency, and players were only given a couple of tops to last the whole season. This was even the case for the 1973 FA Cup final, when at half time, and presumably wanting to change into dry shirts, Bobby Kerr, Dave Watson, Micky Horswill and Dennis Tueart all had to switch from long to short sleeves.

Old kits would regularly then be retained for use on the training ground or to be handed down to the club's reserve or youth sides, but things have relaxed somewhat in recent times and now the club or individual players will often auction or make available match-worn kits for charity purposes, with the British Legion and of course, the Foundation of Light both being regular beneficiaries and seeing their logos adorning commemorative kits.

Additionally, since the 2018 opening of the foundation's superb Beacon of Light facility, the venue has welcomed countless recreational and budding players proudly wearing their own Sunderland strips for a kickabout or training session.

That passion for the club and the area is often in evidence. The centre sits behind the Stadium of Light, between Keir Hardie Way and Vaux Brewery Way, so named to recognise the relationship the club had with the firm. The closure of the brewery in 1999 proved highly controversial and when it was mooted that parent company the Swallow Group would take over the kit sponsorship, fans rallied against the idea of the Lads displaying the logo of a company being accused of causing local job losses. Instead, another successful Wearside brand, the car dealers Reg Vardy, took over the sponsorship.

A bit like the 'candy stripe' shirt introduced in 1981, even now the Vaux story and subsequent wrangling over the usage of the site will stir up some emotive comments from Wearsiders. When in 2021 it was announced however, that a new footbridge was due to be constructed between it and the Sheepfolds site next to which the Stadium of Light sits one of the main reasons for it was to further connect the centre of Sunderland to the ground. The project reflects the club's position as a continued focal point for the city and so do the kits; it was noticeable that the artist's impressions of the bridge featured several people wearing red and white shirts.

As well as shirt sponsorships, the Stadium of Light era has coincided with a period where football clubs have become more alert to the marketing opportunities that are available, and with spending regulations now being imposed, it is important that clubs augment their income through increased commercial activity.

Fans may pine for simpler times, but with results taking precedence there is a general acceptance that for a club to be successful on the pitch, it must be well run off it, and as well as seeing parts of the ground renamed at various points due to different deals, there was even a period in the 2010s when Sunderland had an 'official grooming and skincare partner' in Nip+Man.

Sunderland now have back of shirt and back of short sponsors too and the sale of replica kits can further boost revenues, so when in 2020, Nike became the first company to have a third separate stint supplying the club with first team kit and the first to have more than one at the Stadium of Light, fans were keen to see what the biggest sportswear firm on the planet would be serving up.

The current deal is in conjunction with Spennymoor-based Nike partner, Just Sport Pro Club, whose sister brand Avec produced the first batch of corresponding baby-sized strips, Avec having of course also supplied senior Sunderland strips in the past. The 2020-21 strips also saw a new principal sponsor come on board, with Seaham business utilities advisors the Great Annual Savings Group having their logos on the front of the shirts.

There is something comforting about having two County Durham based firms associated so closely with Sunderland's identity. The club and the city are indelibly linked, but for generations, Sunderland AFC was considered to be 'County Durham's club' too. The fanbase is not restricted to those with a local postcode however, and whether in exile or somehow else drawn to the club, supporters are spread far and wide. With fans based in some of the furthest corners of the globe, wandering Black Cats will invariably bump into somebody else wearing a Sunderland shirt and become instant Marra's.

Indeed, Sunderland shirts will be worn whether there s a game on or not, or at the very least some fans will insist on wearing other elements of red and white. During the 2016-17 and 2017-18 campaigns however, the club released 'matchday ranges' that were based on the colourways of the corresponding home and away kits, and this lead to the unfamiliar sight of supporters wearing combinations of blue and white, pink and purple and charcoal and amber accessories featuring the club badge or initials.

These represent just some of the change colours Sunderland have used since leaving Roker. Perhaps unsurprisingly, given the historical links, it is blue that has featured most often.

These have ranged from light shades to darker ones, with the different hues sometimes being given specific names - even if to the regular person on the street, the baltic blue used during 2002-03 probably does not seem all that different to vivid blue, as the 2011-12 strip was described officially, until you held them against each other.

By 2014-15, the tone being used was referred to as being sharp blue, but again, it probably would not be too far away from the shades used for either the 2006-07 or the 2017-18 change strips if you were looking for them on a colour chart.

The kits all differ in other ways, with different collars, sleeve arrangements and other detailing being introduced over the years. The change kits allow designers more freedom, although in 2014-15, the home kits did also see a new colour feature for the first time in over 30 years when the red, white and black was now joined by a new element - gold. Materials have changed too, with thinner fabrics and breathable sections being introduced when producing modern strips that are now often used in conjunction with base layers by some players.

Of course, some Sunderland kits have had better records than others. Not everybody thinks that the strips are a factor in the team's form, but Roy Keane reputedly did, with former players since recalling an incident when he was claimed to have lost his temper about opposition arriving at the Stadium of Light with better kits.

The fashion in which he turned Sunderland around however was striking - days before Keane joined the club, who at this point were being supplied by Lonsdale, punch-drunk supporters sang 'You're not fit to wear the shirt' at players during a dismal League Cup exit at Bury and yet eight months later they were celebrating promotion.

Successful sides can go long periods without defeat, and the paucity of losses during Sunderland's magnificent 1998-99 campaign, which brought the first promotion since moving to the Stadium of Light, meant that the blue away kit that season was not worn for a single defeat. The next promotion in 2004-05 meant that the accompanying change kit also had a strong record, with the white shirts only seeing two defeats, one with matching white shorts and one with the alternative navy coloured shorts. More recently, Nike's blue and red change kit of 2020-21 was not worn for a league defeat until a narrow loss at Blackpool in mid-April.

Other kits may have decent records simply by virtue of not being used regularly, with the white 2007-08 change design only seeing one defeat, that is if you don't count another two losses when the top was paired with the home shorts. That loss was at Liverpool, who during 2012-13, were one of only three teams to beat a Sunderland side wearing that season's blue change option. The Redmen's traditional colours invariably mean a change of strip for the Lads when they visit Anfield, as do those of several other sides.

Clubs like Southampton and Stoke City that also wear red and white stripes present an obvious clash. Sheffield United, another of those teams, took it even further between 1995 and 1997 when not only did they have the same kit manufacturers as Sunderland, they were even sponsored by a subsidiary of Vaux Brewery.

There can be instances too when even the change kit is not suitable, for example in 2010 Sunderland had to re-use their blue change kit from the previous season at Arsenal as the predominantly white away design that superseded it still clashed. The navy clad Lads were outgunned on that occasion, just as the Lasses had been when wearing the same strip as the two clubs met in the 2009 FA Women's Cup Final.

Not all kit clashes are as immediately obvious, but the use of change strips is sometimes at the discretion of officials who need to be able to differentiate between the shorts and socks as well. Traditionalists may prefer to see a side in their home colours unless they absolutely have to change, but in addition to referees, broadcasters can now also ask a team to wear a change kit if they feel it would aid viewers, whilst some suppliers will have clauses in their contracts about how many times a strip should be used.

Due to these variables, it is not always easy to predict what combination of colours Sunderland will be wearing. When Arsenal wore a commemorative burgundy shirt during the 2005-06 season, it meant a rare outing on their turf in red and white for Sunderland, yet both sides wore white shorts. Against old foes Newcastle United however, whilst the teams have on occasions both been allowed to wear their traditional black shorts, other visiting Sunderland sides have worn white or red shorts with their usual shirts, or gone the whole hog and used full change kits instead.

Despite green being almost universally used by goalkeepers for decades, even the stoppers sometimes have to change strips now if there is a clash with their opposite number. When Oscar Ustari became the first Sunderland goalkeeper to save a penalty in the FA Cup during a tie with Hull City in 2014, he was wearing a navy alternative kit because the hosts were also supplied by the same manufacturer and had the same first choice design. During the same game, the outfield players were all allowed black shorts however, although Sunderland did use secondary red socks.

Changes notwithstanding, Sunderland's kits are a major aspect of the club and its relationship with supporters. Christmases or birthdays can be made when a new strip is unwrapped, and the release of a new design is often something people will look forward to with relish, with heated debates then ensuing about the relative merits of it.

Beauty is in the eye of the beholder after all, but every kit will mean something to those putting it on, whether that is a local lad like Jordan Henderson or Grant Leadbitter, somebody that has come through the ranks like Lynden Gooch or one of the many thousands of supporters that has owned a Sunderland top at some point in their lives.

As well as new replicas, official merchandise such as reissues of previous designs or reworkings as items like coasters, mugs, greetings cards and now even face masks all prove popular. Vintage designs feature on many of the match day flags organised by the Red and White Army too, with people associating these kits with enjoyable games or periods that hold personal significance.

The Stadium of Light has already seen more ups and downs than some grounds will witness in a whole lifetime, and the supporters that have remained through thick and thin, both when the Lads were tearing into the opposition and ripping them to shreds or conversely being cut to ribbons themselves, have certainly earned their stripes.

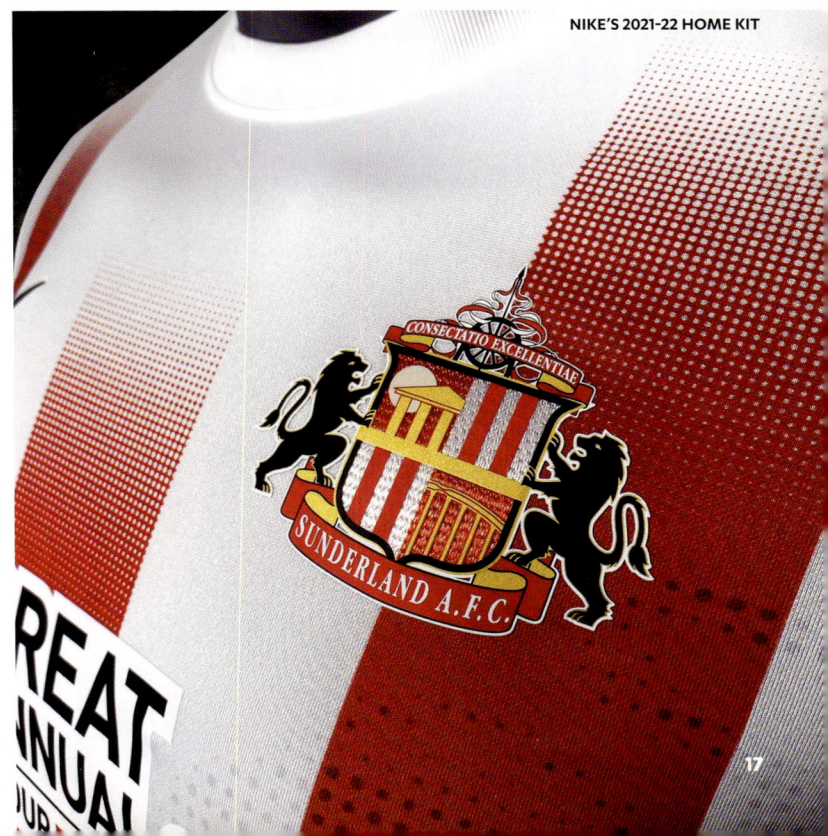

NIKE'S BALTIC BLUE AWAY KIT FROM 2002-03

NIKE'S 2021-22 HOME KIT

1997 98

New stadium, new beginnings. The Stadium of Light era heralded a host of changes on and off the pitch as Sunderland AFC underwent a major change in image.

As well as a new state of the art home, a new club crest was introduced, and the transfer record was almost doubled when Peter Reid brought in Lee Clark as part of his wider efforts to reshape the squad following a last-gasp relegation from the Premier League the previous season. The changes did not end there either, with Reid's new-look side taking to the field in kits provided by Japanese firm Asics for the first time.

The new home, away and goalkeeper kits saw that new club crest placed in the middle of the chest and situated above the logo of Lambton's, which was another new addition to the shirts following the decision of long-term sponsor Vaux to promote their newest brand of beer. The designs also included polo collars that had the unusual quirk of including the makers logo on them, instead of the more familiar placement on the chest, and on the back of the shirt just below the collar the crest was featured again.

The home shirt included a white central stripe for the first time since the infamous 'candy stripe' kit of the early 1980s and was usually paired with solid black shorts that again had the crest on the back, although white shorts were used on occasion. The socks were black with a red turnover. The change kit was a mustard gold shade that was worn with either matching shorts or a navy-blue version, but unlike the home shirt there were no buttons on the collar.

Fans trying to familiarise themselves with their surroundings during the first game at the Stadium of Light also had the unusual sight of seeing Sunderland taking to the pitch in away colours for the second half, although perhaps the kit was best remembered for the unfortunate dark sweat patches that would form under the armpits - fine for the Lads on the pitch but not so welcome when having a few drinks in the new concourses.

It remained a popular shirt with most fans however, as did the home version. Both designs were relatively simple, whereas the goalkeeper's kits were slightly more eccentric, somewhat befitting given the character of regular number one Lionel Perez, with the predominantly bright yellow version including lilac and black patterns and the alternative mainly blue number featuring sections of turquoise and orange. Like so many other things at the club, they were in stark contrast to what had gone on before, as Sunderland entered a bright new world.

SUPERKEV CELEBRATES THE SECOND GOAL IN THE PLAY-OFF SEMI-FINAL SECOND LEG AGAINST SHEFFIELD UNITED

LOOKING GOOD
SUNDERLAND 2-0 SHEFFIELD UNITED
IN TRADITIONAL KIT · WEDNESDAY 13 MAY 1998

Anybody doubting that the Stadium of Light could recreate the Roker Roar surely had their fears allayed on an electric Play-Off semi-final night as the Lads booked a place at Wembley. Roared on by a crackling home crowd and playing some tremendous football, the Lads certainly looked the part on a memorable Wearside evening as they turned around a first-leg deficit to win 3-2 on aggregate.

Feverish activity preceded the first season at the Stadium of Light. As chairman and vice-chairman Bob Murray and John Fickling revealed the name of the stadium in the sports bar at midnight on the night before the opening game, work was still underway to complete the finishing touches of the stadium.

While Murray and Fickling focussed on the completion of what was the biggest football ground built in England in the second half of the twentieth century (even before the north stand extension) manager Peter Reid was looking to build his squad, defender Jody Craddock's transfer being completed on the day the stadium's opening included a blessing by the Bishop of Durham as well as a goalless game with Ajax, along with Status Quo arriving on the pitch by helicopter.

Playing in the grand surrounds of the Stadium of Light re-awakened the sleeping giant that was Sunderland. Roker Park had once been one of the finest stadia in the country, but by 1997, it was a museum piece that would have been better off at Beamish. Chairman Murray was a lifelong supporter who understood what Sunderland were capable of and through his vision, business acumen and determination, he provided the stage for a new era. With Asics providing the costume, Sunderland as a club looked light years away from the one which had ended its almost century-long tenure at Roker Park with relegation.

The 3-1 defeat of Manchester City in the opening home league fixture mirrored the 'Match of the Century' at Roker where City had lost by that scoreline during the triumphant 1973 cup run, but the early weeks at the Stadium of Light were not successful. The second home game was lost to Norwich and only two of the first five home league games delivered three points. Early October brought the 'Nightmare on Elm Park' where Reidy and co were heckled and worse as they boarded the team bus following a 4-0 drubbing that left them in the bottom half of the table after defeat at Reading's ramshackle old Elm Park.

That was a turning point as the Lads embarked on a 16-match unbeaten run that lifted them to fourth in January. Niall Quinn's hat-trick against Stockport County in early March coincided with moving into the top two for the first time, but ultimately and agonisingly the team finished one point short of Middlesbrough in the second promotion place, despite having accrued 90 points.

Condemned to the Play-Offs, Sheffield United were put to the sword in a thrilling second leg before Wembley penalty defeat after a 4-4 draw with Charlton meant the final kick in the away kit was Micky Gray's ill-fated penalty.

LOOKING GOOD
NOTTINGHAM FOREST 0-3 SUNDERLAND
IN CHANGE KIT · WEDNESDAY 4 MARCH 1998

Promotion rivals and eventual champions Forest were cut down to size by an on-fire Sunderland, who won at the City Ground by a three-goal margin for the second season in a row. Goals from Alex Rae, Allan Johnston and Kevin Phillips gave the Lads the points that their gold star performance merited on a balmy evening by the Trent.

ALLAN JOHNSTON JUBILANT AFTER HIS STRIKE AT FOREST

21

1998 99

DANNY DICHIO NETTED A
BRACE AGAINST OXFORD

The previous campaign's popular home kit was used again for this season, but the away kit was another winner with the supporters, having been voted for by the fans themselves.

Towards the end of the Stadium of Light's debut season, supporters were asked to decide between four designs and over 15,000 votes were cast online and at club shops at the stadium itself, in Market Square in Sunderland city centre, The Galleries in Washington, Newgate Street in Bishop Auckland and in the Metrocentre.

The winning design, modelled by defender Jody Craddock, was navy blue with red and white detailing included on the collar, which proudly stated 'Sunderland' on the back, and also across the torso. There was a small red and white label sewn into the front of the shirts and on the back of the shorts that included the club crest, although there was a sight deviation between the prototype and the eventual product, with the detailing on the sleeves altered to match that of the torso, which itself lost one of the proposed horizontal stripes. The navy socks also had touches of red and white, with bands wrapping around the calves. White shorts and socks were worn on occasion.

Craddock's outfit was called 'Strip C' for voting purposes. Of the other three designs, it was closest in look to 'Strip B', which was shown off by Luke Weaver - an odd choice perhaps, as he was a goalkeeper. Weaver's threads also included a red and white collar and torso banding, but was a much lighter shade of blue and had an Asics logo braid running down the sleeves and shorts.

The other two proposals used white as their main colour, with Richard Ord and Nicky Summerbee doing the honours and posing for the camera. Ord, who would then leave the club before he got the chance to wear the new kit, modelled a shirt that had similarities with the preceding away kit with the positioning of the crest and logo, but introduced a blue panel running down the centre.

The designers appeared to enjoy playing around with some ideas, and the Summerbee look had their logo above the club crest with a multi-tone green off-centre braid running down the shirt and shorts. The blue design proved to be a clear winner however and by the end of the season had become the bestselling away kit the club had ever released up to that point.

LOOKING GOOD

SUNDERLAND 7-0 OXFORD UNITED

IN TRADITIONAL KIT · SATURDAY 19 SEPTEMBER 1998

It was a welcome decision when Chairman Bob Murray, as well as announcing the away kit vote, also confirmed that the home shirt was to remain for another season. Also carrying over from the previous season was the free-flowing attacking football Peter Reid's side were serving up, which was at its irresistible best against a visiting Oxford side unable to stem the flow on the banks of the river Wear.

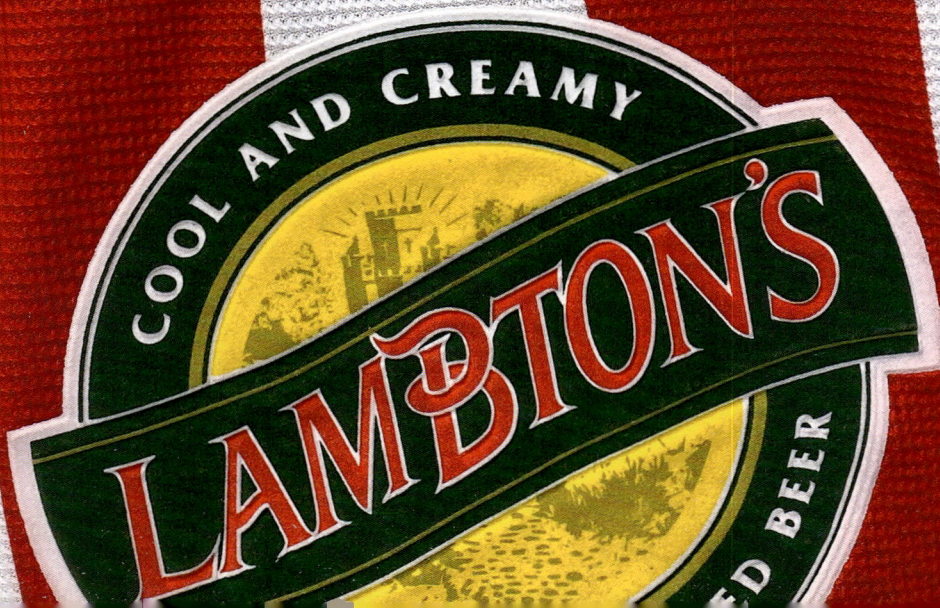

This was the sort of season those lucky enough to witness it will tell their grandchildren about. A record 105 points, although Reading subsequently topped it, were achieved as 31 games were won and only three lost. Despite SuperKev missing four months of the season through injury, nine goals more were scored than in the previous campaign, but the big difference was in defence.

Reid had lost patience with the maverick Lionel Perez after his Play-Off final error and had brought in the great Dane Thomas Sorensen. He also acquired stopper centre-half Paul Butler from Bury, and bolstered by the pair, Sunderland cut the number of goals conceded by exactly a third - just 28 being leaked in 46 games compared to 42 the season before. Incredibly, clean sheets were kept in 30 league games as Sunderland stormed to the league title 18 points clear of runners-up Bradford City. One of those clean sheets was kept at Bradford where after scoring the only goal of the game, Niall Quinn went in goal when Sorensen was injured.

On top of all this, Sunderland even found time to go on a cup run. They reached the semi-finals of the League (Worthington) Cup where they went out over two legs to Martin O'Neill's Leicester City. Victory would have taken the Lads to Wembley where they had lost the previous season's Play-Off in such heart-breaking fashion that it could have derailed a team of lesser characters. Quinn, Reid and ever-popular coach Bobby Saxton had ensured that was not the case. The return home from the old twin towers was not a wake, but the birth of the determination to achieve promotion the following term.

Sunderland started as they meant to go on. Unbeaten in the opening 18 games, of which eleven were won, the response to a shock home loss to Barnsley was to win the next four games, starting with a 4-0 win at Sheffield United where the performance of Michael Bridges persuaded Blades player/manager Steve Bruce it was time to retire.

By the time the return match with Barnsley came around, promotion was already won with four games to spare. A SuperKev special set the seal on a 3-1 win at Oakwell three days after Phillips had bagged four in a 5-2 win at Bury that had sealed promotion.

There would be no let up as even on the final day, with skipper Kevin Ball insistent on everyone still giving 100%, a half-time deficit was overturned as Birmingham were beaten 2-1. This climaxed a season which for the modern generation would be a key part of what would become the good old days in the memories of those there to enjoy it.

LOOKING GOOD

BARNSLEY 1-3 SUNDERLAND

IN CHANGE KIT · FRIDAY 16 APRIL 1999

Having already secured promotion three days earlier at Bury's Gigg Lane, the party moved onto South Yorkshire as the Division One title was secured at Oakwell. Model player Summerbee opened the scoring, Lee Clark broke free to make it 2-0 and after Mike Sheron had pulled a goal back, Kevin Phillips scored a beauty to cap the night off and fully avenge that home loss to Barnsley and leave the hosts feeling blue.

KEVIN BALL CELEBRATES CLINCHING THE TITLE

III 1999
00

NIALL QUINN CELEBRATES SCORING THE FIRST GOAL AGAINST CHELSEA WITH KEVIN PHILLIPS

The choice of home kit for Sunderland's top-flight return was once again opened up to the fans, with there being another four designs from which to decide.

Whereas the previous season's away options were all very different to one another though, the selection this time was not as varied and three of them shared a lot of similar features. That was perhaps borne out with the eventual result, with the more distinctive offering polling more votes than the rest put together and winning with 56% of the vote.

Kits at this point were particularly baggy and would often feature extremely large sleeves, and that was certainly the case with all the options here. Where the chosen design differed however, was by having a 'Grandad' style stub collar, the detail of which matched that on the hem of the sleeves, and by having a horizontal red and white strip running across the back of the shoulders.

Described in the promotional blurb at the time as being inspired by the style of shirt worn by the Sunderland players featured in the famous Thomas Hemy painting that proudly hangs in the main entrance of the Stadium of Light, the kit did include a couple of modern twists too. There was again a small decorative patch sewn into the bottom of the shirts and, perhaps the most well remembered feature, a black cat depicted on the sleeve that football bosses soon decided were not within guidelines for player issue kit.

Subsequently removed or covered with a patch in some instances, the moggies did return with a vengeance when later in the season another fan vote decreed that the 'Black Cats' would become Sunderland's official nickname. Another deviation from the original design was that of the sponsor when, following the shock closure of Vaux, the Lambton's logo was replaced with that of car dealers Reg Vardy, and there was a sting in the tale for the player that first modelled it too - Lee Clark never getting to wear the kit in anger following revelations of him being photographed in an altogether different type of shirt.

New goalkeepers' kits were introduced for the season as well, with black, grey and green options that all included an off-centre red stripe running down the shirts with white piping. The away kit meanwhile was retained, albeit with the new sponsor on instead, and with this being the final year of the Asics deal, the club decided to price home shirts at £29.99 - 25% lower than the previous one.

LOOKING GOOD
SUNDERLAND 4-1 CHELSEA
IN TRADITIONAL KIT · SATURDAY 4 DECEMBER 1999

It is arguable that Sunderland have never looked as good in the modern era as they did on this memorable day, when Niall Quinn and Kevin Phillips both grabbed braces and the team were almost unplayable. There was also a memorable first victory at Newcastle United in 19 years wearing the shirt, but with white shorts, on an evening when snorkels might have been more appropriate given the weather.

Hammered out of sight at Stamford Bridge on the opening day of the season as Sunderland were lucky to get nil in a 4-0 obliteration by a Chelsea side inspired by Gianfranco Zola and Gus Poyet, the Lads responded so well that in the return fixture they were as good as the Blues had been on the opening day.

Chants of '4-0' by the Chelsea fans on Wearside stuck in their throats before half time as Sunderland led by that scoreline with the magical front two of Quinn and Phillips bagging a brace each. Though Poyet pulled back a consolation goal, the performance marked the peak of the Peter Reid era.

Sunderland were fourth in the Premier League at this point in early December and though they went even higher in this season and the next, they never played as well as on the day Chelsea were given such a chasing. There were plenty of other good days however. Earlier in the season three consecutive away games brought two 5-0 wins and a 4-0 victory. SuperKev struck a hat-trick as Derby were beaten 5-0 on their own patch. Three days later the same scoreline was achieved in a cup-tie at Walsall even without the regular front two. When the next trip brought a 4-0 Premier League win at Bradford - having won at home in between - Reidy's kings were flying without wings. Second in the table, a point behind Manchester United, Sunderland were not in a false position.

Having taken four points from the first four games - three of them from a home game against Play-Off winners Watford - the tide had turned on Tyneside. On a night of a storm of biblical proportions, the Black Cats took over as north east top-dogs. The nineties had seen Kevin Keegan's 'Entertainers' bring joy to Newcastle while Sunderland had struggled.

Now it was the red and white's turn to come out on top - goals from Quinn and Phillips overturning a half-time deficit. Magpie manager Ruud Gullit was sacked in the aftermath, while winning the derby gave Sunderland such belief it began a ten-match unbeaten Premiership run.

Shortly after the sensational win over Chelsea, a 2-2 home draw with league leaders Manchester United was a thrilling game that saw Sunderland give as good as they got in a top of the table clash. United were fortunate it was one of two games that Phillips missed. Unleashed on the top-flight, Phillips became the Premiership and Europe's top scorer - netting 30 goals while Quinn's 14 was more than the rest of the team managed. The Lads eventually finished seventh, level on points with sixth-placed Villa. It was Sunderland's highest position since 1955.

LOOKING GOOD

WALSALL 0-5 SUNDERLAND

IN CHANGE KIT · TUESDAY 21 SEPTEMBER 1999

Sunderland, albeit with alternative white shorts, 'blue' away Walsall in the second leg of their Worthington Cup tie and secured an 8-2 aggregate victory with goals from Danny Dichio (2), Eric Roy and Carsten Fredgaard, who scored his only two goals for the club. Also featuring that night was triallist Marcus 'Bica' Di Giuseppe, who replaced Neil Wainwright as Sunderland again walked over their opponents just four days after battering the Rams, Derby County, 5-0 in the league.

STEVE BOULD WITH ARSENAL'S THIERRY HENRY

29

2000 01

Sports apparel giants Nike commenced a second stint as Sunderland's kit manufacturers, meaning that alongside the continued presence of main club sponsor Reg Vardy, the Lads now proudly bore the logos of two companies with large bases in the city at Doxford International Business Park.

With the North Stand expansion complete in time for the new campaign, it was boomtime on Wearside, and to make things better, fans looked swish wearing the 'swoosh' after the release of a very smart set of new kits. Football shirts at this point were still loose fitting, but Nike provided the club with a very unfussy look in the form of a relatively traditional home kit and a stylish away option.

That traditional home design included full red and white stripes on the front, back and sleeves, a simple v-neck collar with red and black detail and black shorts and socks with thin red piping. The change kit also had the same piping on the shorts and socks, but had a polo neck collar and was a brilliant white colour. Incorporating Nike's patented lightweight Dri-fit polyester material technology designed to take moisture away from the skin, the shirts were expected to boost performances on the pitch and meant they had a shiny, bright appearance.

The goalkeepers too were kitted out in straight-forward attire. Thomas Sorenson's famous derby-day penalty save from Alan Shearer that helped Sunderland secure a 2-1 victory over Newcastle United in the November of this season was the undoubted highlight whilst wearing it, but the design itself, with a round collar and black panels under the arms, remained in the background. Tommy was wearing a sage green version that day, but should they have been required there were also off-yellow, dark navy and slate grey alternatives, all with plain dark shorts.

Ironically, given the number of options available to Sorensen and his understudy Jurgen Macho, the all-white change kit did lead to some issues. The black home shorts sometimes had to be brought back out to avoid colour clashes and at Southampton the side wore a bespoke navy-blue shirt as a one-off.

Exactly the same as the regular away kit in everything but colour, the blue version was not available for retail, but holds fond memories for supporters that witnessed Kevin Kilbane pirouetting brilliantly to score the only goal of the game, as SAFC became the last ever away team to win a league game at the Dell - just as the Saints had been the last visiting side to win at Roker Park four years earlier.

LOOKING GOOD
SUNDERLAND 1-0 ARSENAL
IN TRADITIONAL KIT · SATURDAY 19 AUGUST 2000

This was a day for debuts; as well as the North Stand extension being open for the first time and the new kit making its competitive bow, two new boys made their first appearances for the club in a pulsating game settled by Niall Quinn's header. Jurgen Macho quickly showed himself to be up to the task after coming on for an injured Sorensen, but it was an imperious Stan Varga display that stole the show.

Second season syndrome was not an issue for Sunderland. Having finished seventh in the FA Carling Premiership in the first year after promotion, the Lads repeated the feat. This was despite a sluggish start and a run of just one win in twelve games in the spring.

While the defence tightened up, particularly away from home where 14 fewer goals were conceded, the forwards found things tougher. While only six players in the league scored more than SuperKev - including Marcus Stewart, then of Ipswich - Phillips managed fewer than half the goals he had scored the previous season. Similarly, Niall Quinn saw his tally halved. Thankfully, Sunderland had signed a goalscoring midfielder in Don Hutchison who got eight plus another two in the cup.

The fifth round was reached in both cup competitions while in the league the Lads were not just boosted by Hutchison, but also the arrivals of new record signing Emerson Thome and his fellow South American Julio Arca. As the campaign kicked off with a 1-0 win over Arsenal, it appeared Reid had pulled off another stunning piece of transfer business as Stanislav Varga was immense at centre-back. Unfortunately, the Slovakian was injured in the second match at Manchester City, missed over two months and was never as good again.

Up to mid-November, almost all of the early stages were spent just below the half-way mark of the league before Tommy Sorensen's late penalty save from Alan Shearer secured victory at St. James. This sparked a sequence of four successive wins and eight in ten that took the team to second in the table. At this point, the Lads boasted an unbeaten home record of eight wins and three draws. Shortly after, leaders Manchester United ended that run on a night when three players were sent off. Michael Gray was first to an early shower for his protests when referee Graham Poll missed Andy Cole's handball as he scored the game's only goal. Cole was then sent off along with Alex Rae, with Roy Keane and David Beckham having to restrain Cole after his dismissal.

Having lost just one in twelve going into that top-of-the-table clash, Sunderland started a bad patch winning just one of the next ten, the last of the sequence being a home draw with Newcastle when French right-back Patrice Carteron scored Sunderland's goal with a cracker.

Having extended the North Stand, a season which saw the Stadium of Light boast the third highest average gate in the country ended brightly with seven points from the last nine. Kevin Kilbane's clever goal inflicted Southampton's last defeat before leaving the Dell with Kevin Phillips then hitting the winner at home to Charlton. This left the Lads with a chance of qualifying for Europe if they could win the last match at Everton, but a 2-2 draw and results elsewhere meant the Lads just missed out.

LOOKING GOOD

CRYSTAL PALACE 2-4 SUNDERLAND · AET

IN CHANGE KIT · WEDNESDAY 17 JANUARY 2001

Sunderland avenged their Worthington Cup exit to the Eagles earlier in the season by knocking them out of the Axa FA Cup. Strikes from Quinn and Kevin Phillips were not enough to secure progress within 90 minutes, but Phillips scored again in extra time and despite seeing Danny Dichio sent off Kilbane put the gloss on things for the men in white on an evening so cold that Sorensen had to add tracksuit bottoms to his kit.

ALEX RAE CONGRATULATES NIALL QUINN ON SCORING THE FIRST AT PALACE

2001 02

Although Sunderland retained their Nike home kit from the previous season, there was a new star in the stripes following the signature of 'Captain America' Claudio Reyna before Christmas.

Reyna added real quality to the midfield following the unexpected departure of Don Hutchison earlier in the season, but Hutchison's move to West Ham United was only after he had taken part in some of the promotional work for the new away kit. Although native to the north-east, Scotland international Hutchison was an appropriate choice of model given that the kit featured large swathes of what marketing referred to as royal blue and obsidian 'Scotland' blue.

The choice of the two blue tones was in homage the club's original colours when playing their early games at The Blue House Field in Hendon and the heritage of its founder James Allan, who unlike Hutchison was born in Caledonia near the town of Ayr. The kit then got an early outing in a pre-season friendly north of the border at Celtic and came complete with blue shorts and socks.

The design also included a couple of small red details such as on the collar, which the press release stated was a 'performance neckline' with reduced bulk for smaller moisture gathering areas and increased comfort. No stone was left unturned seemingly, and following FIFA instruction that players could no longer wear shirts outside their shorts, Nike also introduced a curved hemline to 'reduce the bulk which is tucked in'.

Red was also used for the letters and numbering on the back of the shirts. At this time, generic sports outlets were usually only able to provide black decals, and so the club shop could proudly boast of an exclusive name and numbering service in red for supporters that wanted to look like the players on the pitch.

One fan that got even closer to the players than normal this season was Colin Lynch, who won a Hays Travel sponsored competition the club ran called 'One of the Lads'. His prize saw him handed a token one-year contract at Sunderland and he was given squad number 73 - another reference of course to the club's heritage and a famous day when another Scot, Ian Porterfield, played a starring role.

For the goalkeepers there were three new options to choose from, all paired with basic black shorts and with the same template including substantial shoulder and elbow padding being used each time, but featuring different colourways. There was a black and grey version, a yellow and orange and a two-tone green, which all had panels underneath the chest area that switched shades and wrapped round to the sides and underneath the arms.

CLAUDIO REYNA

LOOKING GOOD

BLACKBURN ROVERS 0-3 SUNDERLAND

IN TRADITIONAL KIT · WEDNESDAY 26 DECEMBER 2001

Sunderland looked off colour for large parts of the season, but they still raised some Christmas cheer over the festive period. Four days after beating Everton, a Niall Quinn brace and a last-gasp Kevin Kilbane goal beat Rovers on Boxing Day where home defender Craig Short was sent off for wrestling with Kevin Kyle. Victory had the Lads sitting in the top half of the table, but it was to be one of only two doubles achieved all season and the slide soon gathered pace.

Fifth in the Barclaycard Premiership after Kevin Phillips scored his 100th goal for the club in a 2-0 win at Bolton as September ended, it seemed as if the Lads were set for a third successive season in the higher reaches of the top flight. Unfortunately, this was not to be the case.

Don Hutchison had left after a derby draw at Newcastle in August and attempts to replace the ageing Quinn were doomed, new signing Lilian Laslandes proving such a dismal disappointment that Niall ended up astonishingly appearing in every game, 14 of them as sub.

With only one point gleaned from the next four games after SuperKev's landmark goal, Sunderland slumped to 15th and from then on the team would never go more than two games without a defeat. Peter Reid strengthened in mid-season with the joint-record signing of USA captain Claudio Reyna and the acquisition of Cameroon legend Patrick Mboma on loan. Come the end of the season, they were two of six players who played at the FIFA World Cup in the Far East having played for Sunderland that season, along with Great Dane Tommy Sorensen and the Irish contingent of Quinn, Kevin Kilbane and Jason McAteer.

Evidently, there was quality in the squad, but unlike in recent seasons that quality couldn't produce consistent form. Back-to-back wins at Christmas briefly lifted the Lads back into the top half, but two days after a best of season 3-0 win at Blackburn the wheels came off at Ipswich, as the Tractor Boys were 4-0 up by half-time and added another after the break.

Remarkably, just two years after possessing the most lethal front two in the league, Sunderland were the division's lowest scorers, the entire team netting fewer than Phillips had managed on his own during 1999-2000, SuperKev this time scoring eleven of the meagre total of 29. Thankfully, the defence were doing better, conceding significantly fewer than anyone else in the bottom six. Notably, of Sunderland's ten victories only the last; a Reyna inspired 2-1 win over Leicester, was not accompanied by a clean sheet, six of the wins being 1-0.

On the final day of the season, Sunderland could have gone down had Ipswich pulled off a surprise win at Liverpool and the Lads had slipped up at home to already relegated Derby, along with a four-goal turnaround in goal difference. Thankfully, Ipswich lost at Anfield while the point the Lads took from the Rams saw them reach the 40-point mark. Regardless of the drop in entertainment and league position, the average attendance of 46,745 was once again the third highest in the country.

LOOKING GOOD

BOLTON WANDERERS 0-2 SUNDERLAND

IN CHANGE KIT · SATURDAY 29 SEPTEMBER 2001

A former Sunderland player was manager of the opposition when the Lads visited Bolton Wanderers, but the big story here was not Big Sam Allardyce. This was Sunderland's first win in their blue kit and the headlines went to Kevin Phillips as he notched his 100th league goal for the club, with notable mentions too for Thomas Sorensen, who saved a penalty, and Jody Craddock, who scored his first goal for the club.

KEVIN PHILLIPS HOLDS OFF BOLTON'S GUDNI BERGSSON

||| 2002 03

Released to great fanfare on the opening day of the new season, Sunderland reported record sales of their latest home kit over a big launch weekend.

Radio commentator and fan favourite Simon Crabtree was on hand to entertain the crowd as supporters queued up overnight outside the Stadium of Light club shop to be the first in line to get their hands on a shirt that featured a central red stripe for the second time in a row and a large solid red panel that went across the bottom half of the back and round to the sides.

In addition to Crabbers, there was a ball juggler showcasing his skills and an interactive show in the mobile PlayStation 2 dome to be seen, whilst manufacturers Nike hosted a 'Scorpion Football' tournament with teams playing in a replica of the 'Cage' that had featured in their advertising campaign for that year's FIFA World Cup. Anybody that attended the launch and bought the top was given a complimentary mini kit as an extra bonus.

A new away kit was also introduced for the season and this was made available to buy at the end of August with another high-profile event prior to a home game against with Manchester United, with shoppers able to meet some of the first-team squad prior to the start of a match that would see debutant Tore Andre Flo grab the equaliser in a 1-1 draw.

Flo, a Norwegian international himself, had joined an already cosmopolitan squad. Marketing for the new kits featured full England internationals Michael Gray and Kevin Phillips, South Americans Emerson Thome and Julio Arca, and two players from the recent World Cup in the form of Claudio Reyna and Jason McAteer.

Continuing the international theme, the arrival of Mart Poom in November 2002 alongside Thomas Sorensen, Thomas Myhre and Jurgen Macho meant the club had four full international goalkeepers on the books, which was handy seeing as there were four kits for them to pick from. All using the same design but with different colourways, there were illuminous yellow and orange versions with dark detailing plus a grey and yellow, and a black and grey option.

The grey choices were appropriate given results on the pitch. Reyna and McAteer had posed in what was advertised as a 'baltic blue' away shirt, again quite apt given the weather often experienced on Wearside, but it was the cold reality of relegation that would be felt come the end of the season.

LOOKING GOOD
SUNDERLAND 2-1 LIVERPOOL
IN TRADITIONAL KIT · SUNDAY 15 DECEMBER 2002

A late goal from Michael Proctor handed Sunderland their first competitive home win over Liverpool since 1958. Gavin McCann, had earlier given the Lads the lead. Coming just a month after Jurgen's famous 'Macho Man' performance to get a point at Anfield, the win took Howard Wilkinson's side out of the relegation zone, but would prove to be the new manager's last league victory.

Finishing fourth bottom the season before was a warning. The Peter Reid era came to a close early in the campaign. The middle section was calamitously overseen by Howard Wilkinson and by the time Mick McCarthy came in to take the last nine games, the fact that all were lost only added to an already abysmal run.

Sunderland propped up the table with a measly 19 points, with 18 of those gained before Christmas. In the last match before Santa arrived, two second-half goals from SuperKev earned a draw having been 2-0 down at West Bromwich Albion. At that stage, Sunderland were out of the bottom three, but just a solitary point was taken from the second half of the season, and that from a home goalless draw. Only second bottom WBA equalled the 65 goals conceded while only 21 were scored, eight fewer than the second worse Baggies. Phillips top-scored with six, plus three in the cups,

The cups brought a modicum of relief. The League Cup brought a stunning 7-0 away win to Cambridge in Peter Reid's penultimate game, before under Wilkinson, the side came back to win 3-2 having been 2-0 down at Arsenal before going out at Sheffield United. Two hurdles were also jumped in the FA Cup. During the run when only one league game in 19 was not lost, fellow Premiership sides Bolton and Blackburn were beaten after replays - Wanderers after extra-time and Rovers in a penalty shoot-out. Watford ended the run with a fifth-round win on Wearside.

The cup win over Bolton marked the debuts of the expensive Argentinian Nicolas Medina and young Irishman Sean Thornton. Medina actually did okay but was never picked again, but Thornton's willingness to try to create led to him being voted Player of the Year despite only playing 14 games. That was six more than Niall Quinn who came off the bench in eight early season games but announced his retirement after Wilkinson's first game in charge. Niall signed off by donating a car to be given away as a prize in the match programme in the first home game after the announcement.

That match against Spurs was won 2-0 with one of the goals scored by Tore Andre Flo, a record signing who represented the latest attempt to replace the totemic centre-forward. Flo was such a flop that the joke was that the club shop had run out of the letter P as supporters flocked to doctor the shirts that had had the Norwegian's name printed on.

Flo scored just four times including a debut goal that earned an early season home draw with Manchester United three days after a 1-0 win at Leeds. There were other good days such as the home win over Liverpool when local lad Michael Proctor scored a late winner. The problem was there were far too few good days in a season where eight of the points were accrued from the nine games overseen by the man who had brought the good times - Peter Reid.

LOOKING GOOD

CAMBRIDGE UNITED 0-7 SUNDERLAND

IN CHANGE KIT · TUESDAY 1 OCTOBER 2002

Reid's penultimate game in charge of the club was a Worthington Cup rout of the U's. Wearing their baltic shade in a city whose university's sports teams are synonymous with their own version of blue, Sunderland gave a first-class performance. Reyna, McCann, Arca, Flo (2) and Stewart (2) did the honours.

JULIO ARCA

2003 04

Fans that bought the home kit the previous season during that record opening weekend of sales got another year's worth of wear out of it, with the design being retained for Sunderland's return to Division One.

The shorts had small red flashes on the sides and a thin red line round the back, and the mainly black socks had red and white stripes down each side. The previous away kit had used the same template for the shorts and socks but in different colours, although for 2003-04, there was to be a whole new look for when the Lads were on the road and there was to be a clash.

The newly designed away kit was once again blue, but this time it was a much darker shade; navy. The white round collar was replaced with a white v neck collar and where the previous version had featured white flashes down the sides this one had red panels under the arms and around the collar.

It was a sleek effort that once again utilised Nike's innovative Dri-fit hydrophobic and hydrophilic fibres and was paired with navy shorts that had red piping down the sides and across the back of the legs, and navy socks that incorporated their swoosh logo, the S.A.F.C. initials and red turnovers.

Turning over a new leaf was exactly what the club needed to do following a painful relegation. Mick McCarthy's new look side were resurgent, and whilst the season would eventually prove to be a case of 'what if' following two unsuccessful semi-final appearances, there was one moment that gave a much needed reminder of how good things could be; goalkeeper Mart Poom's excellent header to salvage a point at Derby County.

Nike provided goalkeeper kits in thee colour combinations that from the front looked a little like a vest being worn over a longer sleeved top. There were black/grey and green versions, but for his goal at Pride Park, Poom was wearing the light blue alternative.

Later in the season came the sad passing of Bob Stokoe, a man whose impact was reflected when local brewers The Double Maxim Beer Company released an ale in his honour - some of the proceeds of which went towards the ultimately successful 'Statue for Stokoe' appeal. Poom's moment in blue had already led to another local firm, the Darwin Brewery, producing Poominator Ale, and whilst Sunderland were certainly evolving it was not until the following season that fans could toast promotion.

LOOKING GOOD
SUNDERLAND 1-0 SHEFFIELD UNITED
IN TRADITIONAL KIT · SUNDAY 7 MARCH 2004

The cover of Red and White for this FA Cup Sixth Round tie featured Jeff Whitley in the home shirt paired with the alternate white shorts. The run had taken on extra significance following the death of Stokoe, the man that had reintroduced black shorts following his appointment as manager in 1972 and after Tommy Smith's early goal in this match there were high hopes for more cup glory.

Kevin Kyle and Marcus Stewart were the new look Niall Quinn and Kevin Phillips, both of whom had played their final games in the previous season. Clearly Kyle and Stewart were nowhere near as good as Niall and SuperKev, but then again who could be?

Following in the footsteps of such a legendary partnership was the toughest of tasks, but the new look front two scored 16 each in all competitions as Sunderland reached the semi-finals of the Play-Offs and the FA Cup.

Ultimately, the season ended in disappointment, defeats in both semi-finals coming with a touch of bad luck. The underside of the bar thwarted John Oster in the FA Cup while referee David Pugh somehow managed to miss a blatant foul on goalkeeper Mart Poom as Darren Powell scored a last-minute equaliser to take the Play-Off encounter with Crystal Palace into extra-time. The Eagles went on to win a penalty shoot-out in which Jeff Whitley's run-up would have been comic if the outcome wasn't so tragic.

Poom had earlier come up with the greatest moment of the season. A legend at Derby County, the Estonian 'keeper not only scored at Pride Park, but did so with one of the best headers Sunderland have ever scored. That goal in September brought a dramatic equaliser in a game the Lads had thoroughly deserved to win rather than scrape a point.

After starting the season with back-to-back defeats that felt like punches to a boxer already on the floor - as they took the run of consecutive defeats carried over from the previous season to an incredible 17 - the turnaround had come when the team were looking good at Preston.

Having broken the spell, things changed rapidly. After following up victory at Deepdale with a home win over Watford, the re-energised side went to Bradford and won 4-0 with the highlight being a stunning goal from Julio Arca. The Argentinian cult-hero ran two thirds of the pitch before exquisitely chipping 6' 6" goalkeeper Mark Paston.

Mick McCarthy had carried out major surgery to his squad in the summer. Relegation meant the end of an era for almost all of the players who had brought the good times under Peter Reid. While he had experienced the toughest of starts after taking over from Howard Wilkinson, McCarthy had performed something of a miracle in changing a losing mentality into a winning one. Suddenly it was fun to go to the match again instead of it being an ordeal. 2003-04 would see the team derailed at the end, but the foundations had been set for the following season that would see the former Republic of Ireland manager produce a Coca Cola Championship-winning team on the most modest of budgets.

LOOKING GOOD
PRESTON NORTH END 0-2 SUNDERLAND
IN CHANGE KIT · SATURDAY 23 AUGUST 2003

It could be said that this was one of the most important wins in Sunderland's history. A hangover from the previous season meant that defeat here would see the club suffer the ignominy of equalling Darwen's Victorian-era record for consecutive league defeats. Wearing their blue top and substitute white shorts however, Sean Thornton and Marcus Stewart's goals hypnotised a Deepdale team which included Paul McKenna and Michael Jackson, and ensured that the bad record would not be matched.

SEAN THORNTON

45

║║║ 2004 05

Described as using 'technical' fabrics and production processes, the company came up with what could be described as quite busy outfits with several add-ons and features such as heat transfer logos near the hem and the S.A.F.C insignia on the back just below the collars. The home shirt also featured a white panel across the shoulders to aid player identification and, for the first time ever, the club were able to offer female supporters specifically made cuts and sizes.

The home attire had a red collar and white central stripe. Paired with black shorts and socks, these featured a trim design that was carried through to the training kit range and repeated on a white away kit that could be worn with either white or navy shorts that tied in with the navy collar detail and small mesh inserts running from the armpits.

Anybody digging out their old kits will notice that, if they look closely, the stripes on the home kit for this campaign are serrated at the edge and the material is slightly ribbed. The away shirts were more your typical polyester mix, but the goalkeeper kits were also woven differently and felt a little thicker.

The stoppers' shirts also saw the manufacturer's logo and the club crest moved into the central area, but it too retained the trim detailing and had similar mesh slits to the away tops. With four different goalkeepers between the sticks at one point or another during 2004-05, there were three versions of the design; a green one, a black one and a grey one.

Despite two of those goalkeepers, Michael Ingham and Ben Alnwick, both being rookies and having to make their league debuts in the final run in, Sunderland conceded less than a goal a game and looked good at the back for most of the season. In fact, they looked champion; Mick McCarthy's table toppers were dressed for success and a fruitful partnership with Diadora appeared to be on the horizon.

MARCUS STEWART SCORES FROM THE SPOT AGAINST PALACE

LOOKING GOOD

SUNDERLAND 2-1 CRYSTAL PALACE

IN TRADITIONAL KIT · SATURDAY 8 JANUARY 2005

A section of the North Stand roof sustained damage during heavy overnight gales prior to this FA Cup tie, but Sunderland were still able to storm the Palace and secure their first ever Stadium of Light win against a side from a higher division. There was plenty of needle in a match between two sides in Diadora threads following the previous season's Play-Offs and it was settled by Marcus Stewart's cool penalty kick, which came courtesy of a foul from 'one-size' Fitz Hall.

DIADORA

REGVARDI

As in 1998 and 1999, Play-Off penalty defeat was followed up by winning the league. While Mick McCarthy's men were not as good as Peter Reid's 105-point team of '99, the magnificent 94 points they accrued was the second highest in the club's history.

Still reeling from the aftermath of the 2003 relegation, which saw over 20 players leave, the recruitment had to be spot on. It was. Stephen Elliott, Dean Whitehead, Liam Lawrence, Danny Collins, Steve Caldwell and Carl Robinson were brought in for a total of under £600,000, albeit the first three of those players were subject to further payments depending upon appearances.

'Sleeves' Elliott dove-tailed with Marcus Stewart, the pair top-scoring with 15 and 16 league goals. Collins came in after impressing at the Stadium of Light for Chester. He spent the season on the fringe of the side, but the others rarely missed games while other stalwarts included Julio Arca, who scored nine, Stephen Wright and George McCartney, who occupied the full-back berths, and captain Gary Breen who provided a solid central defensive partnership with Caldwell. Eleven players appeared in at least 35 league games including Chris Brown who made most of his off the bench.

None of these were goalkeepers, although for most of the campaign Norway and Estonia internationals Thomas Myhre and Mart Poom provided the last line of defence. Injuries meant that at the business end of the season, Michael Ingham briefly took over in goal before teenager Ben Alnwick came in for his debut on the day promotion was won with a 2-1 home win over Leicester, Caldwell scoring the winner with a towering header.

A sluggish start had seen Sunderland 17th after six games. As happened the season before when Marcus Stewart scored as the record losing run ended at Preston, Stewart was behind the revival. His hat-trick in a 4-0 win at Gillingham sparked a sequence of four successive victories, climaxed by a Carl Robinson winner at Leeds that propelled Sunderland up to fourth.

After the next fixture was lost at Sheffield United there was then just one defeat in ten as the Lads climbed to third by the beginning of November. The year ended with Elliott and Stewart bringing a 2-1 win at Nottingham Forest. This took the team briefly into the automatic promotion positions, but it wasn't until the end of February that they got there and stayed there. Topping the table in early March, a month later they went to promotion rivals Wigan, backed by a sell-out midweek away support of 7,400, and won 1-0, Stewart again the scorer. After clinching promotion against Leicester, the icing was put on the cake with goals from Arca and Elliott as Play-Off-chasing West Ham were beaten at the Boleyn Ground before the trophy was lifted following a 1-0 home win over Stoke in front of a packed out Stadium of Light.

LOOKING GOOD
CREWE ALEXANDRA 0-1 SUNDERLAND
IN CHANGE KIT · SATURDAY 12 MARCH 2005

At first glance this might not seem an obvious choice, but this was a classic example of McCarthy's men playing within themselves in the first half before upping the tempo after the interval - a tactic that served them well all season. The only goal came just before the hour through Stephen 'Sleeves' Elliott who on this occasion was wearing, well, the long sleeve version of the away kit with the darker shorts.

DIADORA

REG VARDY

STEPHEN ELLIOTT

49

LIAM LAWRENCE & FULHAM'S WAYNE BRIDGE

Sunderland went into their 2005-06 Barclays Premiership campaign full of optimism on the back of an impressive promotion, but a late change of kit manufacturer proved to be an ominous sign.

The arrangement with Diadora was due to last another five years, but over the summer, a dispute between them and their distributors lead to an abrupt parting of ways. Lonsdale therefore stepped in at short notice, but the season, like that initial kit deal, would still come to a very disappointing end.

It was not for the want of trying, but on the pitch the players struggled for form. Whilst results were not good though, the fans must have at least felt that the Lads looked the part, with the club able to report strong numbers for an away kit that outstripped the previous version's total sales for the whole year in just the first three weeks of sale.

That away kit saw Sunderland change tack and play in all-black. Made possible by referees in the top-flight no longer wearing black outfits, the kits had silver and red detailing with red piping and numbering on the back. The goalkeeper kits used the same template, with the shorts from the silver version also being used with the away kit when required. There was also a pale blue version for the keepers, and a green option that had red and white detailing instead.

As was the case the previous season, the shirts all had heat transfers near the bottom stating 'Official Licensed Product' and during this era Sunderland were very keen for supporters to buy directly from club stores or online, stating regularly in match day programmes and Legion of Light articles that this would ensure that the money spent would stay inside the club. Adult shirts were priced at £32 and to further encourage fans to use club outlets, anybody that bought an away kit was given a free reversable mini kit.

Due to the earlier issues, the home kit did not go on general sale until the 5th of October. This time the gift for those buying from the club was a SAFC emblazoned football and on that evening the club staged a reserve team fixture at the Stadium of Light with free entry to try and entice more people in. Four days earlier, the first team had just made it four games unbeaten and were starting to look like they were finding their feet, but they slipped into the bottom three after their next game and never recovered.

LOOKING GOOD
SUNDERLAND 2-1 FULHAM
IN TRADITIONAL KIT · THURSDAY 4 MAY 2006

Lonsdale are London based and Sunderland's only Premiership win of the season on home soil happened to come against a side from the capital. This was their final chance of avoiding the ignominy of going a whole season without a Stadium of Light league victory, with the Lads making the most of it after the original game was famously abandoned due to heavy snow after the weather had got so bleak, it was hard to tell just what kit the players were indeed wearing.

Returning to the Barclays Premiership, Sunderland suffered relegation again, breaking their own unwanted record for the fewest points in a Premiership season. Having managed just 19 points in 2002-03, this time a meagre 15 were managed. Given that just a single point had been gained in the last 19 games of 2002-03, this meant that only 16 points had been gleaned from 57 Premiership games come the end of 2005-06.

Three of these came from the last home match. A 2-1 victory over Fulham saved Sunderland from becoming the first team ever to fail to record a home win in a season. They had snow to thank. The original home match with Fulham had been abandoned with the Londoners leading. As of the end of 2020, this remained the only Premier League game to be abandoned due to bad weather.

The red and white army remained unstinting in their support. While not every player could be commended for commitment, those that played regularly certainly could. Sufficient quality was evidently lacking, but the likes of Nyron Nosworthy, Danny Collins and Dean Whitehead commanded the support of the crowd due to their unquestionable desire.

The same could be said of goalkeeper Kelvin Davis. To say he didn't have a good season would be an understatement, but like the black knight in Monty Python's Search for the Holy Grail who loses his limbs in a fight, but insists it 'Tis but a scratch' and keeps coming back for more punishment, Davis refused to take the easy way out. Eleven minutes into his debut on the opening day of the season, Kelvin got his angles all wrong to leave a gaping gap for Charlton's Darren Bent to score in what proved to be a 3-1 defeat.

Eventually taken out of the firing line after conceding four second half goals, including one from 45 yards, to fellow strugglers Portsmouth, the easiest thing in the world would have been for Davis to happily pick up his money, keep his head down and be content to sit on the bench. He would have none of it though and after a five-match absence was back in the side, staying there for the rest of the season. Nicknamed 'Calamity Kelvin' due to some of the clangers he dropped - notably when Michael Chopra scored in a SoL derby - Davis at times was inspired. Sunderland had been effectively as good as down for ages before the night it became mathematically certain at Old Trafford. On that occasion, title-chasing Manchester United were looking not just for three points, but a boost to their goal difference. However, even with fire-power in the form of Ronaldo, Rooney, van Nistelrooy, Giggs and Solskjaer, they could not score as Sunderland retained some pride with a goalless draw under caretaker manager Kevin Ball, who had taken over from Mick McCarthy.

Also leaving the stage was the club's longest-serving chairman Bob Murray who departed having left the legacy of the Stadium of Light and Academy of Light.

LOOKING GOOD
MIDDLESBROUGH 0-2 SUNDERLAND
IN CHANGE KIT · SUNDAY 25 SEPTEMBER 2005

The away kit was worn for two of the season's best performances - on the night where, although relegation was confirmed, Sunderland had battled so hard under caretaker Kevin Ball to secure a point against Manchester United, that the tireless Chris Brown was physically sick beside the pitch such was his exertion, and when Tommy Miller and Julio Arca goals meant a most welcome Tees-Wear derby win.

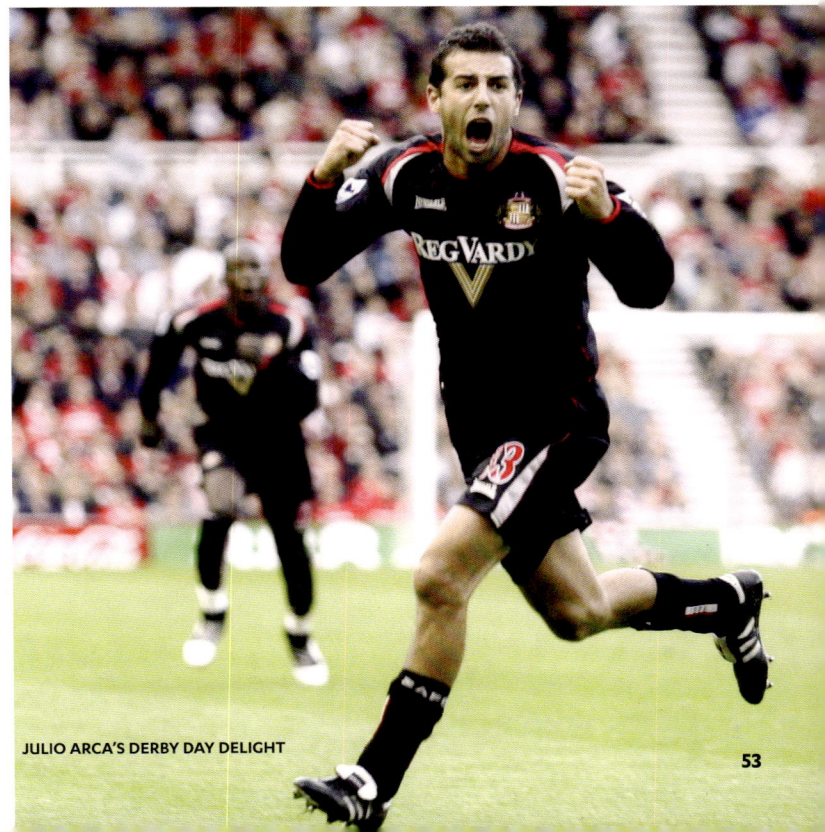

JULIO ARCA'S DERBY DAY DELIGHT

2006 07

This was the last time to date that a home kit was retained for a second season. The shirt had a round neck collar with a small elasticated insert, raglan sleeves and a white central stripe. Whilst the shorts were fairly standard, the socks were black on the front, but the areas that went over the calves were red instead. During both seasons, the side wore white shorts when required - these were the same design as the regular shorts, but instead of the white trim, the extra detailing was also red.

The home kit was one of the few things that stayed the same over the summer following relegation. The Niall Quinn led Drumaville Consortium took over the club and given the number of Irish members the group had, it was something of a surprise that the new away kit was not green. Of the seven new shareholders, only one was not from the Emerald Isle; John Hays, the much-loved Wearside businessman who sadly passed away in late 2020.

There were plenty of Irish connections too on the playing staff, headed up of course by proud Cork man Roy Keane following his appointment as manager in late August. Never known to shirk a fight in his life, he helped pick the club up off the canvas with the team firmly in the blue corner when wearing their new change kit, which was another simple but attractive design.

Mainly sky blue with navy trim and mesh panels sweeping round to the back of the shirt, the kit could be worn with either corresponding sky blue or navy shorts. The socks were navy with sky blue turn-ups that had 'SAFC' running across them and the gift this time for supporters buying direct from the club was a matching gym bag.

Unlike the home kit, which was still embossed, the Reg Vardy logo on the away shirts was a heat transfer application. This was the case with the new goalkeeper kits too, and whilst the pale blue version from last season was carried over, a new design was also introduced featuring either pale yellow and navy sleeves or a rarely seen black and orange option.

LOOKING GOOD
LUTON TOWN 0-5 SUNDERLAND
IN TRADITIONAL KIT · SUNDAY 6 MAY 2007

From dismal relegation to a thrilling title win, no other Sunderland kit of the modern era could be associated with such contrasting form. The final outing of the design, albeit with the alternative white shorts, saw Sunderland clinch the Coca-Cola Championship in style with goals from Anthony Stokes, Daryl Murphy (two), Ross Wallace and David Connolly. The fight back was complete, and this was, to date, the only time the club had immediately returned to the top division following relegation.

DAVID CONNOLLY WITH GOAL NUMBER FIVE AGAINST LUTON

New ownership in the shape of the Niall Quinn led Drumaville Consortium brought almost instant success. The Coca-Cola Championship was won after an initial hiccup.

Unable to appoint the big name manager he and his backers wanted, Quinn took the reins himself early on, before persuading Roy Keane to take on his first managerial role after the team made a desperate start.

Arriving just before the closure of the transfer window, Keane made Sky Sports News seem like a Sunderland special as Dwight Yorke, Graham Kavanagh, Liam Miller, David Connolly, Ross Wallace and Stan Varga swept into town, Varga returning for a second spell having previously played for Peter Reid.

Beginning with a bang with wins at Derby and Leeds, the 'Roy-volution' then slowed for a while, leaving the Lads still in the bottom half of the table as 2006 ended. The arrival of Jonny Evans (on loan) and Carlos Edwards changed things. Evans was partnered with Nosworthy in central-defence as Edwards began his own goal of the year competition with a series of screamers.

A sequence of 14 wins and three draws rocket-boosted the red and whites to the top of the table as Keane instilled his winning mentality. The manager blew a fuse after winning 4-2 at Sheffield Wednesday where he felt his side slackened late on, while on the next trip to South Yorkshire, players were left behind when late for the team bus on the way to Barnsley where Sunderland won nonetheless.

The final home game was a fabulous match full of drama and spectacular goals as Burnley were beaten 3-2. Top-scorer Connolly showed the bottle to convert a penalty after failing with one earlier as Sunderland came from behind to secure three points that took the team to within a whisker of promotion. The winner from Edwards was as sensational a goal as you could wish to see as the Trinidad & Tobago international smashed a scorcher. Even Keane allowed himself a momentary fist-pump as the TV cameras captured Niall leaping out of his Chairman's seat as the weight of responsibility seemed to tumble from his shoulders.

When Derby lost at Palace later the same weekend, Sunderland's promotion was secured, as was Steve Bruce's Birmingham. On the final day, Bruce's Blues were expected to seal the title, but slipped up at Preston while Sunderland went nap at Luton to finish top. Unlike in 2005 when under Mick McCarthy there was an open-topped bus tour, Keane proclaimed that for a club of Sunderland's stature merely winning promotion was not something that warranted the open top bus leaving the garage. Instead, the trophy was presented at a private ceremony at Seaham Hall.

LOOKING GOOD
SOUTHAMPTON 1-2 SUNDERLAND
IN CHANGE KIT · MONDAY 9 APRIL 2007

Wearing all sky blue, Sunderland were flying high after two stunning late goals from Carlos Edwards and Grant Leadbitter put the Black Cats top of the table for the first time in the season. From such a low starting point, the Lads had relentlessly chased down the leading pack with their resurrection peaking over a gloriously hot and sunny Easter weekend.

CARLOS EDWARDS & GRANT LEADBITTER

2007 08

Preparations started early. Roy Keane's Sunderland were big news and with the 2006-07 promotion charge in full swing the club were able to agree two new deals for the coming campaign.

April 2007 saw the announcement that Irish bookmakers Boylesports would become the club's first non-local sponsor. The firm were also installed as Sunderland's official betting and gaming sponsor, and so took over the running of all the match day betting kiosks and facilities.

A month earlier, Umbro had been confirmed as Sunderland's new kit manufacturers after Lonsdale had agreed to terminate their arrangement earlier than planned. A five-year deal was signed with the brand and, buoyed in part perhaps by these new contracts, Sunderland were then able to prepare for their return to the top-flight with a substantial transfer kitty.

Although not 'Bank of England' standards, Roy Keane made several additions to the squad for his first season as a Barclays Premier League manager. Chief among the new recruits was Craig Gordon, who arrived for a British record fee for a goalkeeper.

Gordon was immediately given the number one shirt, which came in either yellow or blue. There was a strong sense of uniformity with the kits, and the goalkeepers used the same template as the outfield kits, all of which were discreetly marked as 'Official Umbro Team Products' and featured matching detailing. The outfield shorts all used the same template too, so there was no need for additional colours to be produced when there was a clash - the home and away ones could easily be swapped over without looking incongruous.

The famous Umbro 'double diamond' was noticeable for being placed slightly higher up on the shirts than usual. It was repeated too on the right sleeves, and on the inside of the collar, the familiar stylised Sunderland prowling Black Cat was a somewhat hidden extra.

The home kit was launched alongside an open training session at the Stadium of Light, which also hosted a Family Fun Day and barbeque on the day the all-white change strip went on sale to supporters. Due to Premier League rules, this away kit then became the third kit the following season and for this campaign, a royal blue third kit was released, but despite being worn for a 4-0 win over Galway United during pre-season it was never used in competitive action.

LOOKING GOOD
SUNDERLAND 1-0 TOTTENHAM HOTSPUR
IN TRADITIONAL KIT · SATURDAY 11 AUGUST 2007

The first Premier League game of the season saw the brand spanking new kit get off to a flyer, as did Sunderland's five debutants. Gordon was alongside fellow new boys Dickson Etuhu, Paul McShane and Kieran Richardson, and was later joined by substitute Michael Chopra, who grabbed a late winner. Also playing, but for Spurs, were six future Sunderland debutants: Pascal Chimbonda, Younes Kaboul, Steed Malbranque, Teemu Tainio, Jermain Defoe and Darren Bent.

MICHAEL CHOPRA'S WINNER AGAINST SPURS

Having struggled horribly in their last two top-flight seasons, this was another tough year as Sunderland sought to cope with the jump in quality following promotion. Manager Keane was backed with over £30m invested in the squad, but most of the campaign was spent in lower mid-table with the team occasionally sliding into the bottom three.

A welcome run of three successive wins in the spring - having previously not managed even back-to-back victories - lifted the Lads to 13th with five games to go. Four losses in the last five fixtures dampened things, but the one win in that run - a thrilling 3-2 home win over Boro - secured safety 50 years to the day since the first-ever relegation.

Safe with two games to go was in contrast with the season as a whole as things were so often left late. Daryl Murphy's winner against the Teessiders was one of eight goals the team scored in or after the 89th minute - the season having started in such fashion against Spurs at the Stadium of Light.

Thirty points were collected on Wearside as Sunderland won more home games than any team outside the top six bar eleventh-placed Manchester City. Full advantage was taken of an inviting run of home games against Bolton, Portsmouth, Birmingham City and Wigan Athletic at the turn of the year as for the first time since 1935 Sunderland won four successive top-flight home games by two goals or more.

Away from home though, Sunderland found it much harder going, with the club record of ten successive defeats being equalled. Only bottom of the table Derby - who took Sunderland's unwanted record of fewest Premier League points - scored fewer than the Lads' 13 goals, or lost more than the 14 away defeats the Black Cats suffered.

Three of those goals on the road came from new boy Kenwyne Jones who scored seven in total to be top-scorer, each one accompanied by his trademark somersault celebration. At his best, Jones was tremendous and contributed to ten other goals in addition to his own seven, meaning that the former Southampton striker was involved in one short of half of Sunderland's modest tally of 36 goals.

The most important thing however, was that after their miserable two previous top-flight seasons Sunderland had survived - and with games to spare. Now there was an opportunity to build.

LOOKING GOOD
MIDDLESBROUGH 2-2 SUNDERLAND
IN CHANGE KIT · SATURDAY 22 SEPTEMBER 2007

Both of Sunderland's away wins came late in the season and were whilst wearing traditional colours. Late goals were a feature throughout however, and a beautiful last-gasp equaliser from Liam Miller gave the Lads, dressed in all white, a deserved point on Teesside. Future Boro favourite Grant Leadbitter had initially opened the scoring before the hosts responded with goals from former Black Cats Julio Arca and Stewart Downing.

LATE JOY FOR LIAM MILLER AND ANTHONY STOKES AT MIDDLESBROUGH

61

2008 09

Fitted football shirts were in vogue again, but Sunderland's new kits still had plenty going on design wise, which was itself fitting given the number of changes taking place at boardroom level, in the dugout and within the squad.

With Ellis Short increasing his presence, Roy Keane set about another summer of considerable squad strengthening. Some of the arrivals went on to give good service and some of them were away again before the end of the January transfer window, yet they still outlasted Keane himself who had departed a month earlier. He was replaced by Ricky Sbragia under whom the club were only mathematically guaranteed of Premier League survival on the final day of the season. Proof, if you ever needed it, that it is never dull at Sunderland - with the kits following suit and offering plenty to talk about.

The home kit featured for the first time in the Stadium of Light era predominantly red socks, a modern twist that contrasted with an away kit that was similar to that of the 2001-02 season, which the marketing stated was again in homage to the early days at The Blue House Field. These were the main points, yet the shirts, and the lime green goalkeeper top that was put with silver shorts, all warranted closer inspection.

The material used was a perforated polyester that, like the season earlier, showcased Umbro's Climate Control technology and their main logos were still placed close to what were elasticated collars. There were mesh inserts on the sides of the home and away tops, trim that went from the armpits to the top of the sleeves, stylised diamond patterns that were repeated on the shorts, and on the inside of the shirts just below the collar was an insert with embossed Black Cats and a bespoke monogram by the hem reading 'Ha'way the Lads'. Even the labels carried an extra, featuring QR codes that took supporters to an exclusive Umbro website with bonus content.

There was a signing session held on the day of the home kit launch, which had first been used on the final day of the previous season against Arsenal, with a family fun day being put on to coincide with the launch of an away kit that was used for the following Stadium of Light fixture, a pre-season friendly against Ajax.

Both games saw 1-0 losses, but it did mean that the Dutch side could now boast the quirky honour of not once, but twice playing against Sunderland in their own back yard whilst themselves wearing red and white.

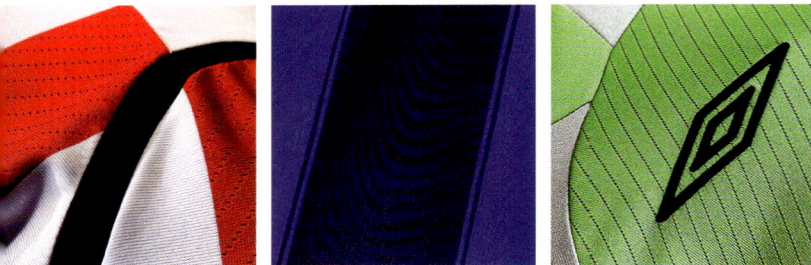

KENWYNE JONES FLIPS OVER HIS FIRST GOAL AGAINST WEST BROM

LOOKING GOOD
SUNDERLAND 4-0 WEST BROMWICH ALBION
IN TRADITIONAL KIT · SATURDAY 13 DECEMBER 2008

Still caretaker manager at this point, this was Sbragia's first home game in charge and a comfortable win started a three-match unbeaten run that saw him given the reins permanently. The Baggies were done by half time following a double from Kenwyne Jones and an Andy Reid header, with Djibril Cisse, Sunderland's number 9, and a man whose style could outshine any kit, scoring from the spot shortly after the interval.

Second-season syndrome was tough, but not a disaster. Sunderland finished 16th rather than 15th as they had the year before, but having been safe with two games to spare in the first season after promotion, this time when losing on the final day they needed results elsewhere to go their way.

An own-goal from Newcastle's Damien Duff brought more than defeat for the Magpies at Aston Villa on the last day. Under Alan Shearer's leadership, Duff's O.G. resulted in relegation while at the SoL, defeat to Chelsea was played in an unreal atmosphere as fans relaxed on hearing the news from Villa Park. Had Newcastle come back to win at Villa, Sunderland would still have survived as Hull City lost at home to champions Manchester United.

A host of new signings included a trio from Tottenham and a couple from West Ham. Coming in from Spurs were Teemu Tainio, Pascal Chimbonda and the mercurial 'Steeeeeed' Malbranque, while from the Hammers came Anton Ferdinand and the returning George McCartney.

Two home wins and an away draw from the first five games saw the Lads sixth early on. By late October, Keane's men were still a healthy ninth after a thrilling 2-1 home win over Newcastle when Kieran Richardson thundered home a rocket of a free-kick to finally end a 28-year wait for a home Wear-Tyne derby win. Given that in the final analysis Newcastle went down when two points behind Sunderland that derby joy was not just about the bragging rights.

Amazingly, manager Keane was sacked at the end of the following month. Six of the next seven games - including a cup-tie - had been lost with owner Short dismissing Keane following a heavy home defeat at the hands of Bolton. That result dropped Sunderland into the bottom three, but many felt Sunderland should have stuck with the Irish legend who had brought the team back from a poorer position the previous season.

Instead Sunderland turned to respected coach Ricky Sbragia. Taking seven points from four games with a goal difference of 8-2 speedily saw Sbragia upgraded from caretaker to manager, but Ricky always seemed reticent about being number one. Nonetheless, he did a sterling job in steadying the ship.

By the end of February, Sunderland had climbed into the top half of the table after a goalless draw at Arsenal extended an unbeaten run to four games. That sequence had included a draw at Newcastle when late on, Chopra had strangely elected to pass to Jones when he had a great opportunity himself, and the chance went begging.

Only one win and five points were accrued from the last 13 games, the sole victory, a key 1-0 win over Hull with Djibril Cisse hitting the winner. He had also scored in both derbies as he finished with eleven goals, but he couldn't quite keep up with the Jones' as Kenwyne collected twelve.

LOOKING GOOD

NOTTINGHAM FOREST 1-2 SUNDERLAND · AET

IN CHANGE KIT · WEDNESDAY 27 AUGUST 2008

Away wins were again hard to come by, with all three Premier League victories on the road coming before new year and whilst wearing traditional colours. The Lads did avoid a Carling Cup upset in their blue change kit however, with Phil Bardsley's late goal forcing extra-time. Debutant David Healy scored early on in extra time to see the Lads through.

DAVID HEALY

2009 10

The final 2008-09 edition of Red and White featured a mean and moody Anton Ferdinand on the cover as he modelled the next home kit. The afternoon saw Sunderland avoid relegation despite losing to Chelsea, and the near miss prompted another raft of changes.

Ferdinand and co were joined by several high-profile recruits with new manager Steve Bruce breaking the club's transfer record to land Darren Bent, who with the new kit now being worn in anger, scored in both of his first two games. The top featured a wrap over collar with matching sleeve hem details and faint embossed crest beneath the main badge.

The kits once again had several extra flourishes that were used across the range. The QR codes were back, and with icons now allowed again, there were small Black Cats underneath the collars. Internally, on the other side of the collars, were lifespan transfers that featured Sunderland's much-loved old ship badge.

Umbro made further use of their Climate Control technology and explained that the shorts, which had tiny internal pockets sewn into them, were also from a lightweight durable woven fabric. The sock turnovers were stylish too, but the big selling point was that the badges on the shirts and shorts were put onto shields, which were sewn on to make the kits smoother underneath and therefore more comfortable for the wearer.

There were some differences though between the home kit and the mainly white away kit, which to the untrained eye was finished with grey sleeves and yellow detailing that was in fact advertised as carbon and sulphur - the reasoning being that carbon is a substance found both in diamonds and coal and that sulphuric acid 'can be devastating'.

The outfield kits had mesh wrap arounds on the bottom of the hems and mesh inserts below the arms, but on the change strip these moved in towards the torso and were included near the small of the back too.

The away tops also had very slight shadow stripes, with the goalkeeping provisions employing two similar templates; one being grey with darker sections across the chest and sleeves, and the other having fewer mesh inserts, but an abstract pattern across the body.

LOOKING GOOD

SUNDERLAND 3-1 TOTTENHAM HOTSPUR

IN TRADITIONAL KIT · SATURDAY 3 APRIL 2010

This was an incident-packed classic. Bent had already seen one penalty saved at Spurs earlier in the season, and yet the fact he had another two stopped by Heurelho Gomes here was not the only talking point, with him tucking away the first spot kick of the game having already snatched the fastest Premier League goal of the season. A late Bolo Zenden beauty then secured the points after Peter Crouch's response, but not before Ferdinand had cause to look all moody again when his celebrations were memorably cut short after his effort was chalked off for a foul.

BOLO ZENDEN'S SUPERB VOLLEY AGAINST SPURS

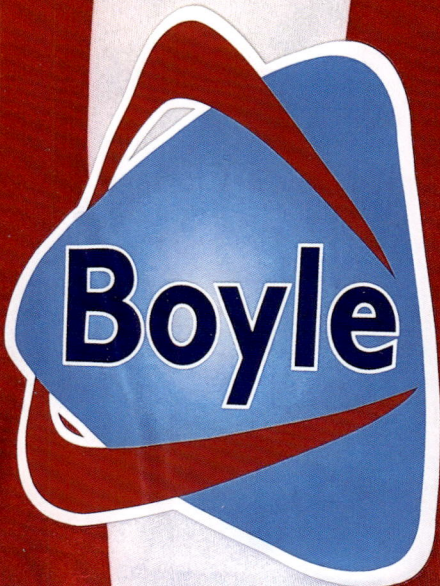

Beach balls were not part of the merchandising, but one thrown onto the pitch by a visiting Liverpool supporter proved to be decisive as a Darren Bent shot went in off it for the only goal of a famous win. Bruce's record buy did not need such luck, as he made his own throughout the season.

Only SuperKev in his European Golden shoe-winning season has scored more Premiership goals in a season for Sunderland than the 24 Darren notched in this campaign, in which he added another against Premiership opposition in the FA Cup.

Backed by the Drumaville Consortium led by Niall Quinn, Bent was not the only big money signing. As well as Fraizer Campbell coming in to bolster the attacking options, a new midfield axis was signed in Lorik Cana and Lee Cattermole.

The combative duo helped the Lads to seventh in the table after the beach ball win over Liverpool with the season almost a quarter old. Injury to Cattermole then restricted the Teesside terrier to just one more league start until late January. By then, Sunderland were on the slide, being midway through a run of 14 league outings without a victory, before Bent blasted a hat-trick against Bolton Wanderers to kick-start a sequence of 17 points from nine games.

A final position of 13th saw Sunderland finish five points above 14th-placed Bolton with a very healthy 14 point gap to the relegation positions. It was an eight point improvement on the previous year and the highest position since 2001 and the second of Peter Reid's back-to-back seventh place finishes. 34 of Sunderland's 44 points were won at the Stadium of Light, but that meant a miserable record of a mere ten being acquired on the road.

Sunderland were so reliant on Bent who scored exactly half of the team's 48 goals, and as an ever-present was the only player to start over 30 Premier League games. Kenwyne Jones contributed nine strikes, but no-one else managed more than four. Overall however, it was an encouraging season as the new manager laid the foundations of a side that would improve the following term even without the influential Cana. The Albanian powerhouse had real presence, but would only spend this solitary season at Sunderland.

LOOKING GOOD
HULL CITY 0-1 SUNDERLAND
IN CHANGE KIT · SATURDAY 24 APRIL 2010

The final points of the season came at a ground Sunderland had helped open eight years earlier when they competed for the Raich Carter Trophy in its inaugural match. There was nothing cordial now however, and a busy first half saw Jimmy Bullard miss a penalty after Bent's early strike via a Kenwyne Jones knock down from an Alan Hutton cross. Loanee Hutton was sent off in first half stoppage time alongside future Sunderland forward Jozy Altidore and although things settled slightly afterwards, Steve Bruce was later sent to the stands for complaining to the officials.

DARREN BENT'S WINNER ON HUMBERSIDE

DANNY WELBECK IS CONGRATULATED ON SCORING THE FIRST AGAINST BLACKBURN BY KIERAN RICHARDSON AND DAVID MEYLER

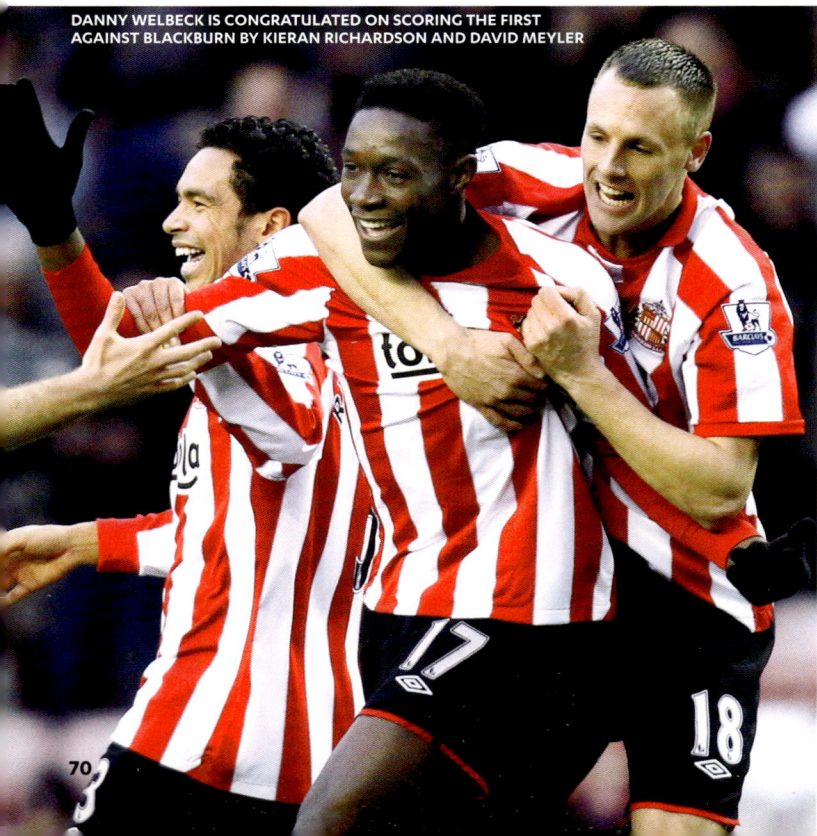

Sunderland's latest set of kits showed a shift in ideas; the team had turned out in some nice efforts in the preceding years, but the new Tailored by Umbro range meant a return to a more traditional look with the home kit especially having a touch of the 1970s about it.

This is not to say the brand new kits were out of date. All including small makers logo inserts near the hems, a patented 'performance fabric' was used and supporters were told they had been ergonomically designed, but in terms of actual appearance things were pared back to a more classic style.

The home shirt featured a polo collar and cuffs, and the red and white stripes were exactly that - if you looked closely you would see that they slightly blurred into one another, but there were no other flashes or features; just full red and white on the torso and sleeves, exactly as the traditionalists would have it. There was an element of red trim, but the shorts design was simple enough too, and with the welcome return of red socks with white turnovers, there was an overall retro feel that could be appreciated by supporters young and old.

The goalkeepers were handed an old school look as well - simple green or blue combinations with shadow stripes, round collars, black shoulders and sleeves, and on the shorts, white trim similar to the home ones.

For the road, the Lads again had understated but stylish kit with a v neck collar and a colour scheme officially described as stone with burgundy trim and shorts. Something that added to the clean look was the fact that the burgundy was used for the sponsors logo too, with online bingo company Tombola starting up a new deal that meant Sunderland were once again in tandem with a large local organisation.

The company were expanding at this point and at the same time sponsored ITV's Emmerdale. It lead to some wags suggesting that the only other thing Sunderland and Emmerdale had in common was that they both made people turn over the channel when they came on, but that was harsh on a side that played attractive football and achieved their third best league finish in over half a century.

Still, Tombola got plenty of exposure. Thousands of complimentary car stickers featuring the kits were made, although another emblem was about to take a back seat. The Black Cat had become a fixture on the shirts and again made a subtle appearance on the inside of this seasons tops, but did not return for the following campaign.

LOOKING GOOD
SUNDERLAND 3-0 BLACKBURN ROVERS
IN TRADITIONAL KIT · SATURDAY 1 JANUARY 2011

On this form Sunderland looked a class outfit. The side worked hard, but it was packed with quality and with the irresistible forward options of Darren Bent, Asamoah Gyan and Danny Welbeck all scoring, the year ahead looked promising. Little did supporters know however that trouble was brewing; Bent had already been angling for a move and come the end of the month his wish was granted.

It wasn't just a new kit that arrived at the Stadium of light over the summer. Steve Bruce's shopping spree brought in ten new faces headed by Paraguay international midfielder who had been bought before the FIFA World Cup kicked off, and so became the first man to score at the finals while on Sunderland's books.

Riveros' next goal would be on his final appearance for Sunderland. That came on the final day of the campaign when he netted the 101st and final goal of Sunderland's Premier League season to complete a comprehensive 3-0 win at already relegated West Ham United. Those three points combined with results elsewhere saw Sunderland jump from 13th to tenth on the final afternoon. It was the first time the Lads had managed to finish in the top half of the table since the halcyon days under Peter Reid.

The win against the Hammers added to a capital record in London. There had been draws at Tottenham Hotspur, Arsenal and Fulham, but best of all was a stunning 3-0 victory at Carlo Ancelotti's league leaders Chelsea. Even without Darren Bent, Sunderland were irresistible and deserved to be ahead long before Nedum Onuoha slalomed through the home defence just before half-time. Second-half goals from Asamoah Gyan and Danny Welbeck made the scoreline a fair reflection of the game on a day when had Strictly Come Dancing been on air, Gyan would have become a leading contender for his 'Babyjet' celebrations.

Despite doing magnificently minus Bent at Stamford Bridge, when the goal machine elected to leave a couple of months later, Sunderland struggled to maintain the momentum they had established. From November until a month after Bent departed in mid-January, a placing of sixth or seventh was maintained, but a slump of just one point from nine games beginning in the second match after Bent went to Aston Villa saw Sunderland slide horribly to 15th.

That run came to an end on the day Jordan Henderson scored twice in a home win over Wigan. The East Herrington lad missed just one game that season - when he was an unused substitute - in a campaign where he made his England debut as a 20-year-old. Sadly like Riveros (and Onuoha, Bolo Zenden, Steed Malbranque and Jordan Cook) that last day win at West Ham United would also mark the last appearance of the Sunderland youngster, who would go on to captain Liverpool to Champions League and Premier League titles.

LOOKING GOOD
ASTON VILLA 0-1 SUNDERLAND
IN CHANGE KIT · WEDNESDAY 5 JANUARY 2011

In one of several balanced away performances, Emile Heskey was sent off for the hosts and with ten minutes left Phil Bardsley turned one point into three when his arrowed strike found the bottom corner. Bolo Zenden, who during the previous away win at Chelsea had memorably exhibited his dance moves, now had to showcase his tap skills; he too was given an early bath after two yellows.

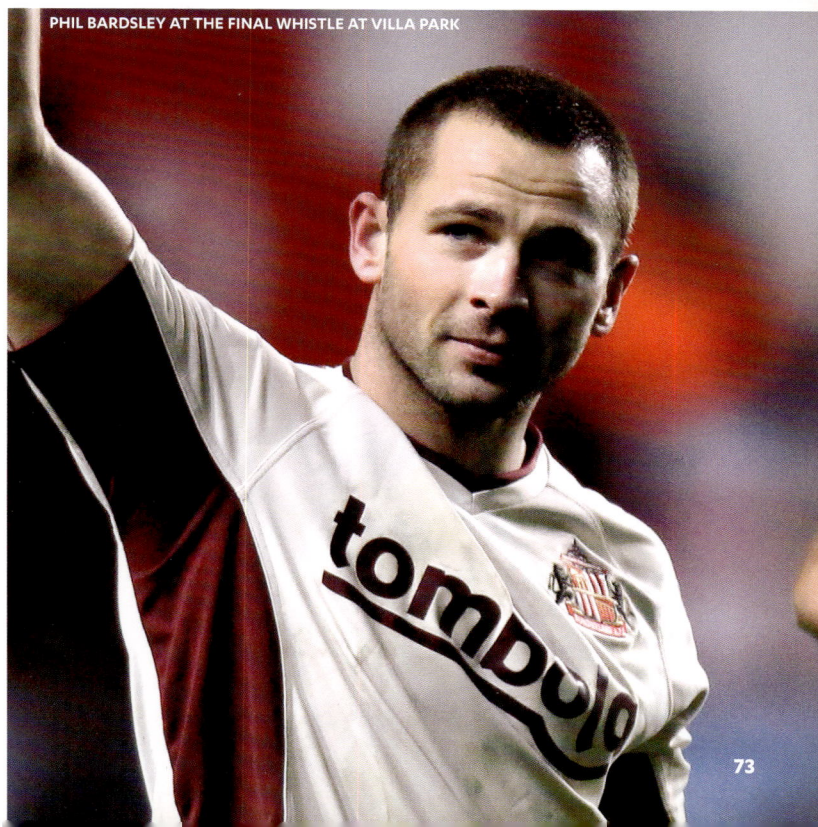
PHIL BARDSLEY AT THE FINAL WHISTLE AT VILLA PARK

73

2011 12

Umbro's 'Tailored by' range brought about another set of uncluttered kits that did the job without fuss, much like summer arrival John O'Shea - a consummate professional who would wear the shirt well for several seasons.

The same could be said for another new recruit, Seb Larsson, who marked his debut with a brilliant acrobatic goal against Liverpool to earn the Lads an opening-day draw.

The game saw Sunderland wear their new away kit, which had been released in July specifically so that supporters could buy it for the summer holiday period. The mainly light blue shirt had a white band across the chest and sleeves that carried the crest and makers logo and went with white shorts and blue socks.

The home outfit was also released early and was particularly smart and straightforward - the only real deviation being that the stripes slid into diagonal chevrons just below the collar on the reverse. The socks were red with white hoops and the shorts, using the same template as the away kit, were standard black with small red trim. They worked well with the top, which had black detailing that again matched the sponsors font - although due to gambling legislation this was not present on baby, infant or junior kits.

Black was utilised a lot, and not just in the sense of caretaker-manager Eric Black, who took charge between the reigns of Steve Bruce and Martin O'Neill. The main goalkeeper's kit was mostly black with a green top strip, and whilst the backup was a yellow top, it had a black collar, shorts and socks.

All the shirts, bar the not-for-retail yellow goalkeeper one, had shoulder panels with repositioned seams for comfort and inserts tucked away with a red, white and black pattern that was repeated on braiding inside the collars. These colours are part of the fabric of the city, and this was reflected in the website address for online kit orders being amended to www.safc.com/fabric.

Go anywhere in Sunderland and you will see evidence of this. Loanee Wayne Bridge reportedly lived near the centre and had he and his pop star partner Frankie spent their spare 'Saturdays' in the appositely named Bridges Shopping Centre, they would have surely seen scores of examples of supporters, who, like stalwarts such as O'Shea and Larsson, know what it means to wear the shirt.

CRAIG GARDNER MOBBED BY TEAMMATES AFTER HIS SWANS STRIKE

LOOKING GOOD
SUNDERLAND 2-1 SWANSEA CITY
IN TRADITIONAL KIT · SATURDAY 21 JANUARY 2012

Manchester City's visit for the previous home game will go down in Stadium of Light folklore, yet one man was certain that this too was a game for the ages. Swans boss Brendan Rodgers' infamous post-match quote that, despite rarely threatening, "It is great for the public here at Sunderland to see us ...we were wonderful" spectacularly missing the point that Black Cats fans attend to back the Lads, not admire the opposition. What they saw were superb finishes from Stephane Sessegnon and Craig Gardner; part of a flurry of brilliant goals scored during this period.

This was the season of the 'Party with Marty' after Martin O'Neill succeeded Steve Bruce. The club parted company with Bruce with after 13 games when a home defeat by the gaffer's old club Wigan left the Lads just two points above Bolton and Wigan who were in the drop zone.

After just nine games under O'Neill, Sunderland had shot up the table to eighth place. Two spectacular late goals from David Vaughan and Seb Larsson turned a potential defeat to Blackburn Rovers into victory as O'Neill celebrated as wildly as might be expected from the newly appointed boyhood Sunderland fan.

For a while Martin certainly seemed to have the magic touch, even inflicting league leaders Manchester City's second defeat of the season, courtesy of a dramatic last-minute goal from Ji Dong-won after City had dominated the game without being able to beat Simon Mignolet whose goalie's kit was added to by a mask as he came back from injury.

As the Lads climbed the table, a cup run got going too. After the Boro's of Peterborough and Middlesbrough were knocked out, Arsenal were beaten in the fifth round to set up a quarter-final encounter at David Moyes' Everton.

Sunderland were good value for the replay they earned at Goodison, but there was the end of an era before the replay. Niall Quinn left the club and the Director of International Development role he had taken on when stepping down from the chairmanship when Ellis Short took on the top job.

With a semi-final at Wembley the prize, the Everton replay simply was not Sunderland's night. A 2-0 defeat saw Stephane Sessegnon volley against the bar and the unlucky David Vaughan score an own-goal as he tried to get back and atone for his own loose pass in midfield. None of the remaining eight Premier League games were won as the side slipped from eighth to 13th. Just three more points would have seen the team finish in the top half.

With Asamoah Gyan departing after the UK summer transfer window closed, the team lacked a regular goalscorer. The on-loan Nicklas Bendtner top-scoring in the league with just eight goals.

LOOKING GOOD
MIDDLESBROUGH 1-2 SUNDERLAND · AET
IN CHANGE KIT · WEDNESDAY 8 FEBRUARY 2012

Having not been on live national terrestrial television since hosting Tottenham Hotspur in 1995, a run in the FA Cup saw the Lads featuring on the box four times in just over two months. One of the games shown was this replay, giving the nation the chance to see the blue away kit in all its glory. Viewers got a bonus half an hour of action when Lucas Jutkiewicz cancelled out Jack Colback's opener to force extra time, before Sessegnon put Sunderland through.

STEPHANE SESSEGNON

2012 13

Prior to the season commencing, Sunderland announced that their new sponsors would be the not for profit organisation Invest in Africa, whose aim was to promote business opportunities on the continent. The club had already confirmed a separate deal that saw new kit providers too, with adidas signing an initial six-year deal that meant Sunderland's would be adorned with the iconic 'three stripes' for the first time.

In contrast to the preceding designs, 2012-13 saw the beginning of a period of experimentation with Sunderland's home look that some felt did not pay off. adidas used their ClimaCool technology, a mixture of heat and moisture controlling materials with ventilation channels and fabrics, and whilst this was intended to improve air flow to the skin and in key heat areas, the designs often strayed from the norm.

Ironically, considering it now bore that stripe motif on the sleeves, the first home kit had fewer actual stripes than usual and the ones it did have were wider. There was a wrap-over collar, which the manufacturers logo sat just underneath, and down the sides were those ClimaCool panels. The sleeves were all red and the socks reverted to black, with the red detailing matching that of the shorts.

In addition to the ClimaCool, the change kit and the goalkeepers kit also had Formotion technology that the designers stated aided body movement and the tops were cut in such a way that the seams did not run directly down the torso. This was a regular adidas feature and such nominal gains can make all the difference at the top level of sport, but more apparent to supporters were the designs themselves, with the away kit a smart navy blue and turquoise combination and the stoppers being offered light blue or orange, both with black sections, and for the adult tops, removable elbow pads.

A hat-trick of commercial arrangements had been sealed when Kitbag became Sunderland's new retail partner, prompting a revamp of the club's online and physical stores. The deals came as the club sought to capitalise on their top-flight status - now established in the Premier League, the end of the season confirmed Sunderland's longest consecutive run in the top division since its first relegation in 1958.

STEVEN FLETCHER

LOOKING GOOD
SUNDERLAND 1-0 WIGAN ATHLETIC
IN TRADITIONAL KIT · SATURDAY 29 SEPTEMBER 2012

Optimism was high before the scheduled first home game. Big money was spent strengthening the squad 24 hours earlier and with away fans being moved into the North Stand a cracking atmosphere was expected. The Reading match was postponed at short notice due to torrential rain however and after that anti-climax, Sunderland never really get going. They drew their first four league games, but when victory did come, courtesy of new boy Steven Fletcher's fifth goal in four league games, it mattered - in the final reckoning, Sunderland finished three points above relegated Wigan.

The 'Party with Marty' evaporated in a season where after starting with four draws, Sunderland flat-lined. With just a single win in the opening ten games, Sunderland were destined for a season spent in the bottom half of the table.

Only once briefly - after a home defeat to Chelsea in December - did the side slip into the bottom three, but they were usually looking over their shoulders rather than being upwardly mobile. Four wins in six games at the turn of the year lifted the Lads to eleventh and the promise of brighter things, but when just three draws added to the points total from the next eight games, owner Ellis Short pulled the plug on the party and sacked O'Neill after a 1-0 home defeat to runaway leaders Manchester United.

At the time, Sunderland were 16th, but just a point above the drop zone having played a game more than Wigan and Aston Villa who were immediately below the red and whites. Shockwaves shot through Sunderland when O'Neill's replacement was named as Paolo Di Canio. A self-avowed fascist, his arrival led to a media furore and the resignation of director, The Right Honourable David Miliband MP. Some supporters declared they would not go back until Di Canio departed and for a while the Durham Miners' Association threatened to remove the Monkwearmouth Colliery Banner from its ancestral home where the Stadium of Light now stands

If there were fireworks off the pitch, there soon were on it as well. After a narrow loss at Chelsea, Di Canio took his charges to St. James' Park and sparked a 3-0 win. Sensational as it was, it should be born in mind that at the time only Wigan and Villa had lost more home games, but it wasn't so much the scoreline as the emphatic nature of it. Always one to want to attack Di Canio was still urging his men forward in the closing stages as he looked to score more rather than protect what he had. Boldness was never in short supply with the Italian whose trousers famously were muddied due to his knee-slide celebrations when Sunderland scored.

While David Moyes' Everton were then beaten in Paolo's first home game as he led the crowd in post-match chants of 'Paolo Di Canio', those victories over the Magpies and Toffees were to be the only ones under the new head coach. Only two points were taken from the remaining four games, the first of those being a 6-1 hammering at relegation rivals Villa. In the final analysis, Sunderland finished three points clear of FA Cup winners Wigan who went down, the Lads being fourth bottom, one place worse off than when O'Neill was sacked.

LOOKING GOOD
FULHAM 1-3 SUNDERLAND
IN CHANGE KIT · SUNDAY 18 NOVEMBER 2012

After beating Wigan, Sunderland's next win came against a handy Fulham side. Wearing blue and playing some incisive football after the dismissal of Brede Hangeland, you would have been forgiven for thinking the Lads were on form, but this was only the second win in 19 league games. Even against ten men things took time to click, but Sunderland responded well to Mladen Petric cancelling out Fletcher's neat finish and pulled away through Carlos Cuellar and Stephane Sessegnon.

CARLOS CUELLAR (HIDDEN) CELEBRATES GOAL NUMBER TWO AT CRAVEN COTTAGE

2013 14

Having ditched the yo-yo tag and now embarking on a seventh consecutive season in the Premier League, Sunderland hoped to capitalise on its place amongst the elite. With the main shirt sponsorship up for grabs again, food distribution business the BFS Group came on board as principal partner in what the press referred to only as a 'lucrative' arrangement. At that point trading in the UK under the name of 3663 and with a depot in Gateshead, the team wore the logo of their large South African parent company Bidvest on their new kits.

Used for a season of soaring highs and desperate lows, those new kits were set to have plenty of memories attached to them. Much like loanee Fabio Borini, not necessarily a great goalscorer but a scorer of great goals, the side could sometimes misfire badly, but then produce some fantastic moments on their day - particularly so in their bright yellow away kit.

The shirt was a simple round neck design with what were described as 'technical cuts and dynamic styling' which featured navy blue detailing and a small amount of salmon trim. Made from adidas' Climalite material, which the company explained was a breathable fabric designed to be worn close to the skin to conduct heat and sweat away from the body.

It was certainly an eye catcher and anybody crossing the road whilst wearing one was probably safer than ever due to the fact they could be seen a mile off. The kit was completed with navy shorts and either navy socks or yellow socks as required.

The goalkeeper provision also had round collars, and the adult versions included removable padding again, with mainly yellow and navy options provided alongside the predominantly green version that was made available for general retail and was finished with several black sections.

It was this one that was worn at Wembley alongside Sunderland's v necked home kit, with Bidvest certainly getting the exposure they wanted as the Lads made their first trip to the revamped national stadium for the Capital One Cup final.

CONNOR WICKHAM WITH CHELSEA'S GARY CAHILL

LOOKING GOOD
CHELSEA 1-2 SUNDERLAND
IN TRADITIONAL KIT · SATURDAY 19 APRIL 2014

Things looked bleak. With games running out and tough opposition looming, head coach Gus Poyet had famously claimed that Premier League survival would be a miracle. Sunderland took their first step to salvation at Manchester City, but an unfortunate late equaliser looked to have deflated the Lads and they were soon trailing here to a Samuel Eto'o strike.
Few people saw it coming. but the ensuing turn around was remarkable; in-form Connor Wickham got the sides level and expert penalty taker Borini sealed the win from the spot to condemn Jose Mourinho to his first Chelsea home defeat in 78 league games.

The novelty of Paolo Di Canio being in charge soon wore off. With Roberto Di Fanti in charge of recruitment, 14 players were brought in, 13 of them on Di Fanti's say so with Duncan Watmore arriving from Altrincham due to the contacts of Academy manager Ged McNamee.

Diminutive Italian international Emanuele Giaccherini from Juventus was a decent player and scored the opening goal of the season, but required time to acclimatise. Meanwhile many of the other new faces looked as if they needed more than simply time to get used to top-flight English football. The likes of midfielder Cabral and centre-backs Valentin Roberge and Modibo Diakite did not look up to the job, although the latter pair excelled in a 1-0 Boxing Day win at Everton. By then Di Canio was long gone, sacked after a miserable one point from the first five games left the Lads propping up the table following the previous term's tame conclusion.

In Di Canio's place - after Kevin Ball held the reins as caretaker boss - came Gus Poyet. So often it has been the case at Sunderland that supporters looked on unsure what the manager was trying to achieve. That was definitely not the case once the 'Gus-Bus' set off. The new head coach wanted to witness 'Poyetry in motion' as he instigated a passing game that saw players drilled to move off the ball, keep possession and play with controlled composure.

Insisting on input into recruitment, amongst Poyet's new faces were his fellow South Americans Santiago Vergini, Oscar Ustari and Ignacio Scocco along with Liam Bridcutt and Will Buckley bought from his old club Brighton. None of these really succeeded at Sunderland. Just as Lee Johnson brought back Aiden McGeady in 2020-21 after previous manager Phil Parkinson had frozen him out, so Poyet re-introduced Phil Bardsley who had been completely left out by Di Canio. Bardo netted the first goal of Poyet's time, but into the wrong net as four second half goals were given away at Swansea. There was much better to come a week later as Fabio Borini blasted a great winner at home to Newcastle.

Nonetheless, for much of the season Sunderland remained in the bottom three or at best just above it. In contrast a great run in the League (Capital One) Cup saw Southampton and Chelsea amongst the opponents eliminated before a two-legged semi-final which resulted in a penalty shoot-out victory over David Moyes' Manchester United, keeper Vito Mannone the hero.

Borini gave Sunderland the lead at Wembley against Manchester City before the light blues ran out 3-1 winners. City also won the Premier League that year and were hot favourites when Sunderland visited them the following month. Sunderland were bottom of the table, seven points from safety with six games to go, but such was the end of season miracle that a stunning run of results against top clubs saw the Lads safe with a game to spare!

LOOKING GOOD
MANCHESTER UNITED 0-1 SUNDERLAND
IN CHANGE KIT · SATURDAY 3 MAY 2014

Just as the home kit was worn against Chelsea for wins in the Premier League and Capital One Cup, the yellow change kit brought both league and cup successes against the Red Devils. The cup semi-final, albeit a magical evening, was a tetchy affair, but the Lads' first league win at Old Trafford since 1968 came following a superb performance in which the Lads played some lovely football. Seb Larsson's winner and victory was a massive part of the survival miracle.

SEB LARSSON'S OLD TRAFFORD WINNER

2014
15

None of this seemed likely during the summer, when Poyet was planning to build on his promising foundations, and Altidore had returned from the 2014 FIFA World Cup determined to prove his worth. The United States international was the only Sunderland player on duty in Brazil, with the tournament commencing the day after the launch of the away kit.

Domestic kits often taken their lead from the advancements and fashions brought about by a major international tournament and Sunderland's newest designs reflected this; the home version was launched two days before the final and following efforts to curb shirt pulling, these were snug to say the least. The goalkeeper outfit was familiar too - Sunderland getting the same design as eventual champions Germany.

Using lightweight and contoured Adizero materials, the keeper options were yellow with purple, blue with cerise and two-tone green. The tops had additional white detailing and long sleeves as standard, although new arrival Costel Pantilimon preferred to cut his and wear it with a base layer.

The home top however, appeared ready made for Defoe, including gold detailing that suited the man whose 'Golden Shot' against Newcastle United helped him towards quickly becoming a modern Sunderland great. The Lads had worn their home kit on Tyneside earlier in the campaign too, but with the alternative white shorts and red socks.

The tops had black mesh panels under the arms and along the shoulders, but the blue away top had them on the shoulders only. It was a smart kit, the first change one from adidas not to have a crew collar, and whilst the idea of pinstripes strikes fear in some fans that recall the early 1980s, the grey and white details on this design provided a sense of that decade but still went down well.

A one-off generic white and blue template kit that was not made available for retail was used in a frantic 3-1 win at Crystal Palace. Sunderland's performance was encouraging, particularly as it was the first away game since being humiliated at Southampton, but Poyet won only two more league games thereafter and was indeed replaced.

LOOKING GOOD
EVERTON 0-2 SUNDERLAND
IN TRADITIONAL KIT · SATURDAY 9 MAY 2015

Sunderland's final league game at Roker Park was against Everton two days after a general election and the same thing happened again here, but whilst it was not quite a landslide the reds did still beat the blues for whom Aiden McGeady was a substitute. Seven days earlier, Jordi Gomez had scored two penalties with unwavering aplomb to avenge Southampton, and whilst Danny Graham and Defoe's deflected finishes here were at the scruffier end of the spectrum, Sunderland fully deserved their only consecutive wins of the season and now had the traction needed to pull out of the bottom three.

DANNY GRAHAM

As in the previous three years, the gaffer in charge at the end of the campaign was not the man who had been in charge when the season kicked off. Gus Poyet was given his cards in March after Aston Villa had taken just 45 minutes to double their season's tally of away goals from four to eight when inflicting a 4-0 defeat. Just over a year earlier, the 'Gus-Bus' had arrived at Wembley, but here it reached the end of the road with the Lads hovering perilously close to the drop zone.

New manager Dick Advocaat became the third gaffer in a row to start with an away defeat and then beat Newcastle in his second fixture. In the Dutchman's case, victory came courtesy of a goal of a life-time from Jermain Defoe. He had arrived in January in one of Sunderland's best ever pieces of transfer business, being swapped for the mis-firing Jozy Altidore.

The experienced Advocaat oozed confidence. Asked in an early Press Conference why he thought Sunderland would stop up, he offered the questioner a withering look and simply stated, 'Because I am here.' He was as good as his word. Quickly gone was the possession based keep-ball that prevailed under Poyet as Advocaat went back to basics. While only one point was taken from the two games after the derby victory, back-to-back wins at home to Southampton and away to Everton lifted the team out of the drop zone with three games to go.

A goalless draw with Leicester concluded the home programme, but left things on a knife-edge as a point for mathematical safety was still required, but with the last two games being at third-placed Arsenal and champions Chelsea. Only Manchester City scored more home goals than the Gunners that season, but regardless of 75% possession and 28 shots Arsene Wenger's men could find no-way through the Wearside defence as Advocaat lived up to his promise with Sunderland safe with a game to spare.

Sunderland conceded the same number of goals as fifth-placed Tottenham, but only second bottom Burnley scored fewer than the Wearsiders' 31. The Clarets were also the only club to match Sunderland in winning just four home games. Connor Wickham and Steven Fletcher top-scored with a modest five Premier League goals each. Defoe netted four, but in the next two seasons would solve Sunderland's striking problem. Wickham would play in all but two of the league games, as would Seb Larsson while captain John O'Shea marshalled the defence, missing just one match.

One thing that could be counted on without question of loyalty was the red and white army. The average attendance of 43,157 was the highest in seven years, with only one of those seasons having dipped below 40,000.

LOOKING GOOD
ARSENAL 0-0 SUNDERLAND
IN CHANGE KIT · WEDNESDAY 20 MAY 2015

Sunderland were draw specialists with their league total of 17 being five more than the next side. The team also had the joint lowest total of wins in the division, so it was fitting that one of the better results, certainly in a kit that only enjoyed one win, a cup replay at Fulham, was another tie. 0-0 draws can sometimes be drab affairs, but there were plenty of heart-stopping moments at both ends as Advocaat marshalled his troops to a battling point that secured Premier League survival.

DICK ADVOCAAT CELEBRATES WITH JERMAIN DEFOE

2015
16

LAMINE KONE SCORES AGAINST EVERTON

Club stores underwent a programme of summer refurbishment following the end of Sunderland's deal with Kitbag, and they were of course soon stocked with a new kit range.

Sunderland could have perhaps released a range of red and white bouquets too when supporters contributed to a fund set up to recognise Dick Advocaat's efforts the season earlier and persuade his wife to let him return. A large bunch of flowers was delivered to Mrs Advocaat and the surplus monies donated to charity.

The shops were not the only thing undergoing an overhaul as the squad again had a makeover. Back in post, Advocaat was given several new recruits by sporting director Lee Congerton, but it quickly seemed that the purchases where not quite what he wanted - despite handing Premier League debuts to six fresh arrivals he was soon gone, and this time for good.

His replacement Sam Allardyce, in addition to his own buys also gave a senior introduction to Jordan Pickford. The Washington keeper had grown up supporting his hometown team and was photographed as a youngster wearing Sunderland kit, and now he was doing it for real.

This was the first time that adidas' goalie offering was not round collared and instead there was a slight v neck with insert featuring on the blue, orange and grey options. The shorts were the same template as the main kits and accompanying training gear, which all had a band running around the back.

Although the subject of a goodwill gesture when those attending the game at West Ham United were given complimentary shirts, the away kit received mixed reviews. Unless you count the teal change kit released when Pickford was a new-born, this was Sunderland's first green outfield kit and not everybody was a fan - not least colour blind supporters with red-green vision deficiency.

Using what was described as a tonal green gradient, the accompanying 'solar pop' mesh matched the black detailing of the home shirt, which used a white base intended to make the stripes stand out. adidas had certainly taken a gamble with the release, which featured the logo of latest sponsor Dafabet, a Philippines-based online bookmaker and gaming operator.

LOOKING GOOD
SUNDERLAND 3-0 EVERTON
IN TRADITIONAL KIT · WEDNESDAY 11 MAY 2016

It seemed like Sunderland had cracked it. Sam Allardyce's team had a defined style and oozed quality, not least across the midfield axis of Jan Kirchhoff, Yann M'Vila and Lee Cattermole. Four days on from a breathless Chelsea show that put Sunderland within touching distance of survival, they made sure of it with an imperious display capped off by goals from Patrick van Aanholt and Lamine Kone (two). Fans headed home hoping for more of the same in 2016-17.

The season had more than a touch of deja-vu about it. Yet again a different manager ended the season than started it, engineered a dramatic and exciting end of season escape - and beat Newcastle in their second game in charge.

Following Dick Advocaat's departure shortly after his wife's flowers had died, Allardyce began at the Hawthorns - scene of Paolo Di Canio's final match just over two years earlier. A sixth successive win over the Magpies - 3-0 at the Stadium of Light - proved doubly invaluable in the final analysis. The red and whites stayed up being one place and two points ahead of the black and whites who went down, the latter derby having finished all square on Tyneside.

Despite that October home win over Newcastle, Sunderland remained in the bottom three and stayed there very nearly all season until March as Big Sam's success in the January transfer window started to bear fruit. Sunderland should have looked for a sponsorship deal with Special K as Lamine Kone, Jan Kirchhoff and Wahbi Khazri transformed Sunderland - with Younes Kaboul hugely influential. As well as partnering Kone in central defence Kaboul was a French speaker who was a major factor in enabling Kone and Khazri to fit in.

Ridiculously labelled a dinosaur, Big Sam in fact was as modern a manager as they come in terms of how switched on he was to sports science including sports medicine. In game after game, former Bayern Munich reserve Kirchhoff would be a towering presence in closely fought games, but two thirds of the way through, his number would be up and the German would come off. Allardyce knew that if he pushed Jan too far he would break down, but by careful management he got the best out of the player. Kirchhoff played 14 of the last 15 games, being subbed in ten of them and was finally rested for the final game at Watford after safety had been secured.

Six goals were scored in the final two home games, three each against Chelsea and Everton. Khazri blasted the goal of the season against Chelsea, but the Lads still had to come from behind to win a fantastic game in which Jermain Defoe scored his 18th goal of the season and John Terry saw red for an injury time lunge at the Tunisian Khazri. Four days later, the Toffees came unstuck as Kone became the first central defender since Sandy McAllister against Bury in 1903 to score twice for Sunderland in a top-flight game. The victory kept Sunderland up, but sent near-neighbours Newcastle United down with Norwich, despite the Canaries winning on the same evening.

As the season ended, Sunderland's last eleven games had brought just a solitary defeat, and that to Leicester City in the sensational season when they became champions having opened the campaign with a 4-2 win over Advocaat's Sunderland.

LOOKING GOOD

SWANSEA CITY 2-4 SUNDERLAND

IN CHANGE KIT · WEDNESDAY 13 JANUARY 2016

Swansea had a man sent off having earlier levelled via a softly-awarded penalty and despite then taking the lead, had no answer for Jermain Defoe's finishing masterclass. Having already scored in the opening minutes, Defoe nabbed the match ball with two further efforts after Federico Fernandez had deflected a van Aanholt punt in to make it 2-2. Swansea claimed two of his goals were offside, but Sunderland having Defoe's prowess in their ranks just made the other clubs in the relegation battle green with envy.

JERMAIN DEFOE WITH THE MATCH BALL IN WALES

2016
17

VICTOR ANICHEBE

Whilst the late survival charges had been thrilling, the constant cycle of managerial and structural changes were not doing any long term good. Sam Allardyce seemed like the man to take Sunderland forward, but there were rumblings of discontent even before England had come calling and so on the face of it, replacement David Moyes looked the next best option.

His tenure was catastrophic however, and ironically, for a club desperate for stability, the first season since 2011-12 that they started and ended with the same manager resulted in a listless relegation; the gold home kit detailing jarring against Sunderland's wooden spoon placing.

The shirt had a central white stripe for the second season running, although adidas did change the socks for the first time since becoming Sunderland's kit manufacturer and introduced a smart red design with black and gold flourishes. The shorts also had gold trim, and here adidas introduced another change - with squad numbers now featuring on shorts their logos switched to the back of the leg.

This detail was carried throughout the range, which included a retailable third shirt for the first time in nearly a decade. Pink and purple, the design featured a monochrome club crest and different shirt and short ClimaCool mesh placement to the other outfield kits. Some could not decide if they liked it or not, but one thing not up for debate was its playing record - seen in competitive action four times, Sunderland did not register a single goal in it, never mind a point. Hardly a purple patch.

The primary change kit did enjoy some bright spots. Anybody that had previously complained about 'only' picking up a point on the road learned to take what they could get; there was only one away draw and three wins in the league, but they did all come in the white design that featured a blue fade diagonal stripe across the chest.

The blue was repeated with the trim and 'three stripes', although for the goalkeepers this adidas staple was instead on the sides as the sleeves featured Aztec patterning. There were bright yellow and green choices, but more appropriately given the prevailing mood, a black one too. Moyes left a day after the season ended.

LOOKING GOOD
SUNDERLAND 3-0 HULL CITY
IN TRADITIONAL KIT · SATURDAY 19 NOVEMBER 2016

Taking until a club record equalling eleventh time of asking, the Guy Fawkes Day victory at Bournemouth was the latest date upon which Sunderland had chalked up a first league win of the season, but with the leaves now falling, it did at least prompt a flurry of points. The Lads won two of their next three outings, including this game where Jermain Defoe scored his 150th Premier League goal, Victor Anichebe grabbed a brace and Papy Djilobodji was sent off. What really lit up the autumnal sky though was thousands of fans holding aloft mobile phone torches when there was a short second-half power cut.

Having finished the previous season strongly, Sunderland backed new manager David Moyes in the transfer market. Over £21m was spent on Didier Ndong and Papy Djilbodji with a further £13m on a pair of double-deals for players from two of the manager's old clubs: Donald Love and Paddy McNair from Manchester United and Darron Gibson and Bryan Oviedo from Everton, the latter pair in January.

Other ex-Evertonians to arrive were veteran Steven Pienaar, Victor Anichebe and Joleon Lescott. Goalkeeper Mika came from Boavista while from Manchester Adnan Januzaj arrived on loan from United with Jason Denayer coming from City, along with Javier Manquillo on loan from Atletico Madrid.

Not amongst these 13 new faces was midfielder Yann M'Vila, the France international who had done so well on loan the previous season and who very publicly made clear his desire to return. Nonetheless, with the club sanctioning such serious strengthening, Sunderland had a squad capable of continuing their decade-long run in the Premier League. This was especially the case considering the new boys added to the backbone of the side which had Defoe up front, Lamine Kone at the heart of defence and Vito Mannone and the up and coming Jordan Pickford offering strength in the between the sticks.

Given a daunting task at Manchester City on the opening day, the Lads looked like taking a point when level with seven minutes to go, at which point Moyes took off Defoe to bring on McNair only for the substitute to put through his own goal. After subsequently losing the opening home game to newly-promoted Boro, manager Moyes was asked if he thought his new team would be in a relegation battle. He replied, "I think that will be case, yes." It was in stark contrast to Advocaat's insistence Sunderland would not go down 'Because I am here' when the Dutch master arrived with nine games to go two seasons earlier.

By the time just two points had been taken from the first ten games, there was no denying the manager's statement, especially as Younes Kaboul had been allowed to leave. But whereas under Allardyce, Advocaat and Poyet there had been determined and successful fights to get out of trouble in recent seasons, in 2016-17 it seemed as if the old guard of John O'Shea and Seb Larsson along with only a handful of others were battling for the shirt.

Inevitably, Sunderland went down, bottom of the league and 17 points adrift of fourth bottom Swansea. A final day 5-1 loss at Chelsea who had already sealed the title was a tame surrender, with none of the fight and defiance the committed, but plainly not good enough team of 2006 showed when being relegated while holding title-chasing Manchester United to a goalless draw at Old Trafford. Whatever the design of the shirt, fighting for the right to be fit to wear it has always been essential.

LOOKING GOOD

CRYSTAL PALACE 0-4 SUNDERLAND

IN CHANGE KIT · SATURDAY 4 FEBRUARY 2017

Cast aside by England, Allardyce was now at Selhurst Park to witness the type of performance Sunderland fans hoped would become a regular occurrence had he stayed. Lamine Kone, Didier Ndong and Defoe (with two) had fans rubbing their eyes in disbelief, but perhaps just as surprised was Jack Rodwell who was finally on the winning side after 38 league starts for the club. Despite all their struggles, Sunderland were not yet adrift and there was hope that the Black Cats had one of their nine lives left, but that notion was extinguished seven days later when Southampton cruised to victory, Fireman Sam's foundations now in ruins.

DIDIER NDONG

2017 18

Celebrations marking 20 years at the Stadium of Light included hosting Celtic for the Dafabet Cup. The firm sponsored both sides and were now joined by energy supplier Utilita, who became Sunderland's first 'back of shirt' partner. The Eastleigh company's logo was on official player issue kit only, although supporters would later become familiar with the town's football team.

This was another arduous season, and for many the home shirt was a bone of contention. Having previously experimented with fewer stripes, adidas went completely the other way and brought in several narrow stripes plus a solid red back panel. When supporters suggested it looked like something a 'butcher would wear' they did not mean Terry.

One welcome feature was the 'for Bradley' insignia added for Millwall's visit, with Sunderland releasing a customised retail version to raise funds for the Bradley Lowery Foundation. Earlier, Dafabet had allowed their logo to be replaced with that of the charity for the Carabao Cup tie against Everton.

The designers explained the multiple stripes paid homage to some of Sunderland's earliest kits. The historical angle was homed in on and the launch event saw local sides Dawdon Welfare Park and Hall Farm Glasshus playing at Ashbrooke Sports Club, the site of The Groves Field which the club used in 1882 and 1883.

The away kit launch harked back even further with Brendan O'Donnell, the great, great grandson of James Allan, proudly revealing the top as he took up his seat for the first game of the season. Light blue and fairly plain, it was nothing extraordinary, but seemed more popular than the home kit.

A bespoke third kit was produced again too. Charcoal and amber to reference the area's industrial heritage and with cuffs like the home kit, another innovative launch saw the Durham Miners' Association Brass Band performing at the Sheffield United game. A stylish kit, it was used twice, a defeat at Aston Villa and a draw with Preston North End.

The kit marketing tag line 'Our future is rooted in our history' was a nice sentiment, but the team were in fact rooted to the bottom for the second season running and suffered a first ever consecutive relegation. The campaign ended with Stewart Donald agreeing to swap Eastleigh for becoming majority owner at Sunderland.

JOSH MAJA'S FIRST SENIOR STRIKE

LOOKING GOOD
SUNDERLAND 1-0 FULHAM
IN TRADITIONAL KIT · SATURDAY 16 DECEMBER 2017

In 2006, victory against the Cottagers meant the club avoided going a full season without a home league win and with Fulham again the opposition, the aim now was to stop it enduring a whole year without one. 364 days after beating Watford, Josh Maja's first senior goal ensured another narrow win and sparked scenes of joy and relief. This was new manager Chris Coleman's fifth game, but neither he nor his short-lived predecessor Simon Grayson ever solved the home form conundrum.

98

Despite all the doom and gloom following the dismal relegation of the previous season, hopes that an immediate promotion campaign might be mounted did not look far-fetched when the team sat sixth after three games due to a cracking 3-1 win at Norwich, in between hard-fought draws at home to Derby and away to Sheffield Wednesday.

The radical change in kit had been matched by a radical change of playing personnel as new manager Simon Grayson handed debuts to six players in the opening fixture. One of those was the on-loan Lewis Grabban who scored twelve times in 19 league games as he showed what a clinical finisher he could be. Unfortunately, by January, he also wanted to end what was intended to be a season-long loan, preferring to briefly return to parent club AFC Bournemouth before swiftly going out on-loan again to promotion chasing Aston Villa. Grabban's loss to Sunderland was measured by the fact that come the end of the season he was still comfortably the Lads top scorer.

Grabban had outlasted manager Simon Grayson who got the bullet on Halloween immediately following a home draw with Phil Parkinson's bottom of the table Bolton. Sunderland were soon bottom themselves and would be at the end of the season by which time Grayson's successor Chris Coleman had also been sacked, coach Robbie Stockdale being asked to take over as caretaker manager for the second time that term.

In a season of calamitous signings, the situation with the goalkeepers overshadowed major problems elsewhere in the side. Having sold Jordan Pickford and Vito Mannone, newcomers Jason Steele, Robbin Ruitter and Lee Camp all endured truly torrid times. Only Ruitter would survive to a second season and in that would make just one further league appearance, as a sub.

Half of the 46 games were lost, more at home than away with former hero Darren Bent scoring as Burton relegated Sunderland with two games to go, Burton finishing second bottom.

In the face of a second successive season propping up their table, Sunderland averaged 27,635 - higher than over a third of the teams in the Premier League. It was the season covered in the first series of the Netflix programme 'Sunderland 'Til I Die.' The Lake Poets wonderful theme tune of that series, 'Shipyards' included the refrain, "I hope that I'm making you proud." Not for the first time, the main thing to be proud about at Sunderland was the support.

LOOKING GOOD

DERBY COUNTY 1-4 SUNDERLAND

IN CHANGE KIT · FRIDAY 30 MARCH 2018

Winless in ten, victory in the away kit against fancied Derby was certainly out of the blue. The season opening reverse fixture in which this kit was launched was broadcast live on Sky Sports and gave the release extra exposure, whilst this match was also televised to a now disbelieving audience. Sunderland started brilliantly, and lead via George Honeyman's deflected strike before Ashley Fletcher doubled the advantage. Unfazed by Matej Vydra's reply, Aiden McGeady and John O'Shea completed the rout.

THE LADS DELIGHTED AT McGEADY'S DERBY GOAL

101

2018 19

With the club entering only its second stint in the third tier, the new regime had plenty to be getting on with, and a swiftly made decision about the latest home kit helped towards getting supporters back on side. The previous season's design had not been popular and although the 2018-19 version was already agreed prior to Stewart Donald's arrival, the original plan to use red shorts as the primary choice was quietly dropped.

These had been a popular alternative previously, but sticking with tradition was seen as seen as the safer choice for the time being. Instead, the black back-up option was elevated, and it was quickly decided that the new look was to be accompanied by one in the stands too, with a collaborative seat change programme adding to the much needed feel good factor.

Another early boost was the arrival of new goalkeeper and eventual Player of the Season Jon McLaughlin. The goalkeeping department had been an issue throughout the previous campaign: Ruiter, Steele and Camp all struggling, no matter which of the plain black, light blue and white variations of their kit they chose.

A green version of the template, not used as player issue was later put on sale too, although none of these kits had the padding, which had been removable from the adult tops that adidas had previously featured. The subsequent 2018-19 designs were very similar, they were cut alike and had the same v neck collars and 'three stripes' placement, although now, the new maroon and black and orange and aqua coloured tops all had a horizontal stripe pattern across the front.

These and all other player issue kit featured the name of latest principal partner, betting exchange firm Betdaq. The deal meant that when Sunderland had to re-use the previous season's blue away design for an eventful win at Bradford City, it had to be updated with the new logo.

Sunderland's actual change kit was black, but the Bantams' home shirts featured black sleeves and a shade of claret similar to Sunderland's red, prompting the switch. Kit completists hoping to get the set were pleased however to see that a small number of the makeshift shirts were made available at a reduced price.

LYNDEN GOOCH

LOOKING GOOD

SUNDERLAND 2-1 CHARLTON ATHLETIC

IN TRADITIONAL KIT · SATURDAY 4 AUGUST 2018

Fans had consoled themselves over the summer with the hope that relegation would at least open the door to some home-grown talent, and with new manager Jack Ross coming into a club short on bodies, a total of ten Academy of Light products were given a first-team debut during the campaign. Three earlier Academy graduates had already started making their way however, and played vital roles in the season, and on a day when newly appointed captain George Honeyman skippered the side, the points came courtesy of Josh Maja and a stirring late Lynden Gooch winner.

The dividing line between success and failure can sometimes be a thin one. Such was the case in 2018-19 when a penalty shoot-out defeat and a goal four minutes into added time brought massive disappointment in the first year Sunderland had made two trips to Wembley.

Supporters filled Trafalgar Square and Covent Garden as well as the national stadium as the Red and White army decamped to London, but while they returned home disappointed, colours were definitely not lowered as a new record average attendance for League One of 32,156 was set, along with the highest individual attendance at that level since the division was renamed in 2004: 46,039 for a Boxing Day win over Bradford City.

The Checkatrade Trophy final attendance of 85,021 was also a record for that competition (and more than that season's League Cup final between Chelsea and Manchester City). Sunderland led from the first half until eight minutes from time and subsequently lost on penalties, but there was even greater heartbreak two months later when a late late goal from Charlton's Patrick Bauer saw the Addicks go up, as they had done when beating the Lads on penalties in a Play-Off final 21 years earlier.

Sunderland probably should not have been in the Play-Offs. For much of the season it seemed as if an automatic promotion spot was on the cards, even though other than for the month of November, and very briefly after beating Burton with six games to go, they did not occupy a top two spot. For much of the season the Lads were on the heels of the leading teams, but with games in hand. However, taking only two points from the last four fixtures in which they lost the last two games, after being defeated just three times in the previous 44, meant that Sunderland finished fifth. Only in a goalless draw at Barnsley, who did go up automatically, did Sunderland fail to score, the home game with the Tykes being a belter, won 4-2.

The turning point came with the January transfer window. As in the previous season the top scorer left. This time it was Josh Maja who was expensively replaced by Will Grigg, a deal publicly viewed in the second Netflix series and one which saw the striker fail to ignite. Since at least the 1950s and the 'Bank of England Club' tag, it has been evident that the size of the fee does not necessarily equate to the success of the transfer, a fact further highlighted by the vast improvement in goalkeeping thanks to the recruitment of free transfer Jon McLaughlin who was ever-present. Under new management on and off the pitch in the shape of Jack Ross and Stewart Donald, Sunderland had come close to a league and cup double, but ultimately it was double trouble as for the first time ever Sunderland faced a second successive season in the third tier.

LOOKING GOOD

BLACKPOOL 0-1 SUNDERLAND

IN CHANGE KIT · TUESDAY 1 JANUARY 2019

After setting the League One attendance record on Boxing Day six days earlier, Sunderland then started the new year in front of a tremendous away following. Over 7,000 of a near 11,000 strong crowd were there to support the men in black, who won thanks to Maja's first-half finish.

LUKE O'NIEN

2019 20

CHARLIE WYKE

Things had been tough previously, but nothing could have prepared supporters for this. Failure to achieve promotion the season before led to something of a hangover and Sunderland struggled for consistency, but when the devastating coronavirus pandemic meant supporters were unsure even when the next game would be, many felt bereft.

Without the structure of the season, its benefits of being a release and an opportunity for social interaction were lost to tens of thousands of fans. When it was then decided that the remainder would be cancelled, a deeply dissatisfying decision to rank teams on a points per game basis left the club languishing in their lowest-ever finishing position. No matter how quickly people accepted the new normal, seeing Sunderland ensconced in the third tier should never sit right.

The halt also brought an early end to another set of kits. The solid red back panels of the previous two home designs were replaced with one of partial stripes, but the shirt was now predominantly white with only three red stripes on the front. There was a small element of black, but the trim was otherwise red, matching the socks.

The new sponsors logo was also red, although this was not always intended to be so. Betdaq opted to gift its sponsorship to Children with Cancer UK, but with Sunderland's outfield replica shirts just about ready to go, thousands had to be altered and the charity's logo quickly placed on.

It worked well with the away kit, a smart blue design adapted from adidas' Tiro 19 teamwear range with pattern detailing and red trim. The adidas stripes were down the sides, as was the case with the goalkeeper's jerseys. The stoppers were kitted out with yellow, green and silver varieties of a swirling print design.

After becoming official bus partner, Stagecoach commissioned vehicles to be liveried with images of the kits and celebrating the new Sunderland AFC Hall of Fame, meaning supporters could now board a bus with a huge image of Charlie Hurley on it; fitting considering his opponents often felt like they had been hit by one. The kit decals meanwhile were obtained during a photoshoot including Max Power and his son, Bali Mumba and Keira Ramshaw alongside other club employees and supporters. Posing near Roker beach, it was part of the 'One Club, Our Club' campaign - by the end of the season many needed to feel that togetherness.

LOOKING GOOD
SUNDERLAND 3-0 BRISTOL ROVERS
IN TRADITIONAL KIT · SATURDAY 22 FEBRUARY 2020

Despite an early demolition of Tranmere Rovers, Phil Parkinson took time to get things going after replacing Jack Ross. Come this game, Sunderland were flying, victory one of four in a row where the Lads did not concede. It was part of a wider sequence of one loss in 15, with Sunderland's high press paying dividends and bringing late goals here for Lynden Gooch, Charlie Wyke and Luke O'Nien. Things looked good, great even, but it proved to be the final win of 2019-20 and was followed by a costly dip.

Children with Cancer UK

Keeping families together

Sometimes seasons seem to fly over. This one certainly did as the last ball was kicked in early March as the season was initially suspended and then ended due to the Covid 19 pandemic. The campaign started well. Three tough games to start with brought draws at home to Oxford and away to Ipswich before a hard-fought home victory over Portsmouth.

Further wins over Rochdale and AFC Wimbledon - the latter with the help of a Chris Maguire hat-trick - elevated the Lads to third. After eleven league games, Sunderland were in a Play-Off place and had also won away to Premier League clubs Burnley and Sheffield United in the Carabao (League) Cup, but manager Ross was sacked after a second defeat of the season, Sunderland having played with nine men in the earlier loss.

Under new manager Phil Parkinson, Sunderland slumped to the club's lowest ever placing of 15th in the third tier after a Boxing Day goalless draw at home to his struggling old club Bolton, but three days later there was a big improvement with a win at Doncaster. That began a run of eight wins in ten games which propelled the Lads into fourth position on the back of eight clean-sheets in those matches.

Just as things were looking up, two home draws and two away defeats took the wind out of Sunderland's sails as the season came to an unexpected halt. No matter that six of Sunderland's eight remaining scheduled fixtures were against teams in the bottom half of the table, a formula was worked out based on points per game. This left the red and whites in a record low final place of eighth while Wycombe Wanderers went on to win the Play-Offs having been elevated back into the Play-Off places on points per game thanks to their early season form, although they had lost over half of their previous 14 league games when the points per game was introduced.

For a few weeks it looked as if the season might re-start, but it soon became obvious that this would not be possible. Sunderland would face another season in League One and supporters would face over a year without being able to go to the match. Given that the Championship and Premier League were concluded - as were the Play-Offs throughout the league and that part-way through the following season, clubs in some areas of the country were allowed to admit 2,000 fans. Sunderland supporters went without seeing their team for longer than most. It was perhaps during this time that being able to wear a Sunderland shirt was all the more important in showing that even in the face of the worst pandemic to hit the earth for a century, the red and white army still wanted to show their stripes.

LOOKING GOOD

MK DONS 0-1 SUNDERLAND

IN CHANGE KIT · SATURDAY 18 JANUARY 2020

Sunderland fans once again travelled in numbers for a game settled by Lynden Gooch's wonder-goal, but it was hardly a bolt from the blue as the Lads had spent the second half ratcheting up the pressure. It sparked wild celebrations, and as the hordes set off back home, promotion was very much a topic of conversation, just as developments in China were becoming a talking point too.

CHRIS MAGUIRE

2020 21

As you read through this book you may have found that a once disliked design has since grown on you, or that a kit you loved at the time now seems dated. The initial responses to the new strips were good however, with the change version in particular seeming to go down well with a fan base of which many were having to get to grips with streaming games instead of attending them.

That change strip featured a dark blue shirt with a red polo collar and red trim on the sides, the detail of which was repeated on the home shorts. With Nike's Dri-fit technology in play again, the red trim, sides and back of the shirt were perforated, whilst the front included a triangle effect micro pattern.

The primary choice of shorts to go with these shirts was red, and these were also used alongside the red sleeved home top for the trips to Rochdale and Plymouth Argyle. During 2002-03, Nike had provided Sunderland with a dark blue back-up option, and they did so again now - neither vintages were seen all that often though, with trips to Doncaster and Accrington Stanley the only instances they were used in this campaign.

There was also a goalkeeper's kit that was only seen fleetingly in first-team action. Although worn slightly more often in academy games, the all silver strip worn by senior stopper Lee Burge in consecutive matches at Blackpool and Hull City was a lot less notable than the bright 'highlighter pen' fluorescent yellow and orange versions that were rotated during the other fixtures. All from the same template and with shirts that again had perforated backs, the strips had round collars and white detailing along the sleeves and shoulders.

All of the kits had plain, single colour socks. For the third time running the home ones were red, although one of standout performances of the season was a 2-0 win at Portsmouth for which Sunderland wore black socks instead.

With all matches bar the two Play-Off games played out in a surreal spectatorless atmosphere, 2020-21 was also the first in an initial two-season deal with new principal partner Great Annual Savings.

AIDEN McGEADY SCORES GOAL NUMBER TWO AGAINST OXFORD

LOOKING GOOD
SUNDERLAND 3-1 OXFORD UNITED
IN TRADITIONAL KIT · FRIDAY 2 APRIL 2021

Sunderland's home form was indifferent for large parts, but they did produce some excellent football at times. In a highly charged game against Oxford, goals from Lynden Gooch, Aiden McGeady and Max Power secured a ninth league win in eleven games and at this point the Black Cats were firmly in the promotion hunt.

The season started at the end for supporters. The final game of the 2020-21 campaign brought the biggest attendance of the year in any of the three divisions of the EFL, but also the lowest crowd to witness a competitive game in the history of the Stadium of Light.

Nonetheless, the 9,971 who saw the Play-Off semi-final second leg with Lincoln City at the end of a period dominated by the global Covid 19 pandemic saw a match which encapsulated Sunderland's season.

It was the first time since March 2020 that supporters had been allowed into the Stadium of Light. Needing to overturn a 2-0 first-leg deficit, the Lads turned it on as they swiftly levelled, only to concede a goal which brought a 3-2 aggregate loss. Sunderland won the game, but not the tie. So near yet so far.

Sunderland's final goal of the term was the 31st by Player of the Year Charlie Wyke. Incredibly, it was also the 30th he had scored with a one-touch finish. Over half (16) of Wyke's goals were headers, including four in one game against Doncaster all of which were set up by Aiden McGeady. Not selected until Lee Johnson replaced Phil Parkinson as manager in December, McGeady ended the season having created more assists than anyone in the league.

Goalkeeper Lee Burge's 18 league clean sheets was the best since Thomas Sorensen's 24 in 1998-99 while the team had never conceded a lower number of goals per game in away games in the league: 0.73 per game compared to 0.78 in 1998-99. Despite these impressive statistics of goals conceded and scored and made by individuals, as a team, Sunderland ultimately fell just short of what was needed to win promotion.

Cause for optimism came in the takeover of the club by Kyril Louis-Dreyfuss with the new chairman's vision for the future being something supporters eagerly anticipated seeing unfold from his first full season of 2021-22 and beyond.

So far in the Stadium of Light era Sunderland seem to have had as many highs and lows as there have been changes in kit. Whatever the footballing fashions, something that has never gone out of style is the loyalty of the red and white army, a fanbase which will always sport its colours with pride.

LOOKING GOOD
BURTON ALBION 0-3 SUNDERLAND
IN CHANGE KIT · SATURDAY 20 FEBRUARY 2021

Seven days after a breathless win over Doncaster Rovers, three days after securing a place in the Papa John's Trophy Final and two days after Kyril Louis-Dreyfus acquired a controlling interest in the club, the Lads completed an encouraging week with a comfortable victory against bogey side Burton. Grant Leadbitter, the red white and on this occasion blue American Gooch, and top scorer Charlie Wyke got the goals.

GRANT LEADBITTER CELEBRATES
HIS OPENING GOAL AT BURTON

1913

ENGLISH (FA) CUP FINAL

SUNDERLAND 0-1 ASTON VILLA

CRYSTAL PALACE · SATURDAY 19 APRIL 1913

The Lads reached their first final in 1913 facing a familiar foe in Aston Villa. The two clubs were early titans of the game and were already battling it out as they both chased a prized league and cup double. The rivalry of the clubs had been immortalised in Thomas M.M. Hemy's 1895 painting which now adorns the entrance hall of the Stadium of Light.

On that occasion the sides wore the colours that they are still associated with to this day - Sunderland in red, white and black and Villa in claret, blue and white. This was the case again for the cup final 18 years later, although it seems as if Sunderland's shirts were now much slenderer and much less starchy, with the design featuring lace collars.

Goalkeeper Joe Butler wore a cap and a light coloured jumper. Butler had the same black shorts and black socks as his teammates, the socks having been updated that season and featured fewer hoops on the turnovers than the previous design.

What Butler did not have was a crest. Badges did not become regular features on kits until much later, but it was fairly common practice at this point for outfield players to bear a coat of arms in the cup final, with the lads displaying the County Borough of Sunderland's emblem on their shirts. The coat featured a sextant in the middle and the town's motto 'Nil Desperandum Auspice Deo', meaning 'with God as our leader there is no cause for despair'.

THE MATCH

It was fortunate that the game took place at all and that the record 120,081 crowd attended without any problems bigger than many of them couldn't actually see much of the pitch. Plans for the Suffragette movement to bomb the grandstand on the day before the match had not materialised although other sporting events around this time were successfully targeted.

The clash of Sunderland and Villa was the first time the cup final had been contested by the teams at the top of the table. On the day of the final Sunderland should have been away to Villa in the league. That fixture was played a few days later, a 1-1 draw helping Sunderland to go on and become league champions.

Villa had slightly the better of the final which was won by a header twelve minutes from time from West Stanley-born Tommy Barber. Villa also missed a penalty which was taken by Southwick-born Charlie Wallace, a former Crystal Palace player who shot well wide, but it was from his corner that Barber scored, just as Villa's Clem Stephenson (another north-easterner, from Newsham, near Blyth) had dreamed. England international Wallace's penalty remained the only one missed in a cup final until 1988.

Sunderland had their chances. Harry Martin hit the inside of the post late on after Sunderland had failed to score when Villa were down to ten men after their goalkeeper Sam Hardy had to go off for treatment. Harry Low's shirt from the final is pictured here. Courtesy of his descendant Maurice Low, it is on permanent display at the Stadium of Light along with Harry's runners-up medal.

NIL DESPERANDUM AUSPICE DEO

1936-37

This was Sunderland's first Wembley visit and London Transport notified supporters travelling to the capital how to get the stadium with large posters detailing which tube stations and bus/trolleybus services to use. Featuring an image of somebody ironing a Preston kit, the artwork also depicted a Sunderland shirt drying on a washing line in the background and whilst reproductions of the poster are a wonderful keepsake, the shirt portrayed was not entirely accurate.

On the poster, the shirt has a granddad collar and long sleeves. In reality, Sunderland's shirts now had a standard button collar and although extremely baggy, the shirt sleeves were approximately elbow length. Worn with the shirts were knee-length black shorts, described then as pants, and black socks with red turnovers that were better known at the time as hose. Goalkeeper Johnny Mapson turned out in a dark bulky roll neck jumper.

Although first seen in the FA Cup in 1933, numbering on the back of shirts was still not commonplace at this point. What did feature on the outfield shirts again however, was Sunderland's updated coat of arms. At this point the design was assumed and the coat was not officially granted until it was updated once more towards the end of the following decade, but the crests still took pride of place.

The kits were provided by A. Lowings sports outfitters of 34 Frederick Street. The proprietor, Amos Lowings, was a cricketer and had previously co-owned a sports shop with former Sunderland forward Charlie Buchan. Another store, Murton's of 16 Fawcett Street, also supplied the club with apparel and subsequently displayed the trophy in their window.

Champions and now cup holders, with a Charity Shield victory in between for good measure, Sunderland were the best team in the land and looked better than ever.

THE MATCH

Both Sunderland and Preston were appearing in their first Wembley final. Frank O'Donnell put PNE ahead seven minutes before half time, becoming only the fourth player to score in every round. He might have had two, only to be unceremoniously hacked down by Bert Johnston when about to go through one on one with teenage keeper Mapson. These days it would have been a red card, but Johnston escaped with a finger-wagging.

Sunderland came back to win with three second-half goals. Bobby Gurney equalised seven minutes into the second half, skipper Raich Carter made it 2-1 from a pass from Gurney who had been Best Man at Carter's wedding the previous Monday, and with twelve minutes left, winger Eddie Burbanks made it 3-1. "That's a nice wedding present for you" said the Queen as she handed Carter the cup.

The shirt featured here was worn in the final by Len Duns. Courtesy of Peter Coates it is on permanent display at the Stadium of Light, along with Duns' winner's medal

1937

FA CUP FINAL
SUNDERLAND 3-1 PRESTON NORTH END
WEMBLEY · SATURDAY 1 MAY 1937

CAPTAIN RAICH CARTER HOLDS THE FA CUP ALOFT CHAIRED BY HIS TRIUMPHANT TEAMMATES

1973

FA CUP FINAL

SUNDERLAND 1-0 LEEDS UNITED

WEMBLEY · SATURDAY 5 MAY 1973

BOBBY KERR
ALL SMILES
WITH THE FA CUP

This is arguably the most famous Sunderland kit ever. The Lads were top to toe in new gear, or that is what we were meant to think anyway. The team were reputedly given, what at the time were, large sums of money to use new Stylo boots, but some of the players have since suggested that they were so uncomfortable they just painted their old ones to look like them instead.

There was no such skulduggery with the kits and accompanying tracksuits, despite Sunderland wearing unmarked outfits during the rest of the cup run. There had been the big change, back to black shorts, following Stokoe's arrival, but the crew neck home shirts had remained and in the semi-final against Arsenal the side wore a relatively plain white kit with red numbering on the back. Now though, Umbro were clearly on the scene.

Stokoe's bright red tracksuit (which is now on permanent display at the Stadium of Light courtesy of his daughter Karen Craven) was one of several iconic memories from the game. As he led the side out, those following were all resplendent in matching tops with large Umbro International branding on one side of the chest and their famous italic font insignia on the other that read 'SAFC'. Below that the text 'F.A. Cup Final 1973' was embroidered, and on the back were their names.

Presentations done, the Lads peeled off their tops to reveal new shirts with a red collar and triangular insert, similar to that of the semi-final, red cuffs and a smaller Umbro emblem. The insignias were on the shirt too, and the shorts had Umbro's diamond logo also. Sunderland's kit was completed with definitive red socks with white turn overs.

Goalkeeper Jimmy Montgomery regularly produced the seemingly impossible: not least in the semi-final against Arsenal when he wore a green top with a similar collar design as the outfield players. His top now was virtually the same, but also had the insignias and logo, and as was often the case, he had what looked like an outfield top underneath.

The match was broadcast worldwide, many watching in colour for the first time. Sunderland's vivid stripes stood out even more then against the grey backdrop and gloomy conditions, and their heroic efforts have remained in the public psyche ever since.

THE MATCH

Thirty-one minutes had passed when Ian Porterfield made 'The Impossible Dream' come true. As with Sunderland's first goal in their only previous Wembley appearance the goal came from a corner. Billy Hughes' cross saw Leeds pre-occupied with Dave Watson only for the ball to come to Porterfield who controlled the ball on his left thigh and smashed it into the net with his right foot.

When Leeds did test Jim Montgomery, 'The Mighty Jim' encapsulated the fairy-tale final with a great double save regarded as the best ever seen at the national stadium, thwarting Trevor Cherry and Peter Lorimer. At the final whistle it was Monty Stokoe ran to, an image now captured forever in the Stokoe statue.

The shirt featured here is from Vic Halom, Sunderland's centre-forward, and is on permanent display at the Stadium of Light.

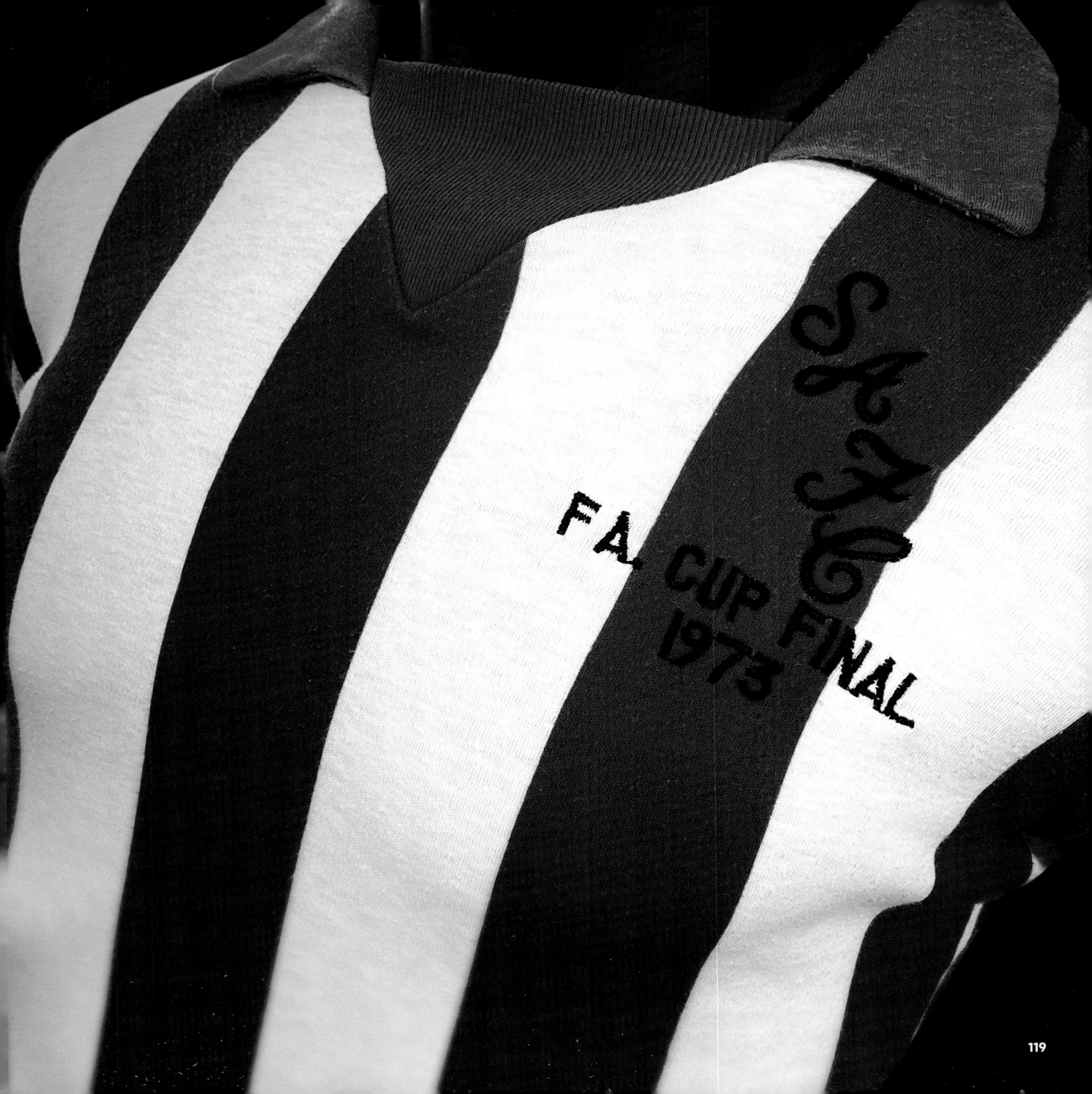
SAFC
F.A. CUP FINAL
1973

This was a final of firsts - it was the first time Sunderland had reached this stage of this competition and it was the first time they had appeared at Wembley wearing a sponsor, but sadly it was also the first time the Lads lost under the Twin Towers.

Sunderland were not the only ones now with a backer, the League Cup itself having been rebranded earlier in the decade after the Milk Marketing Board had become a sponsor.

As well as the block capital lettering font on the shirts, the tracksuit tops Sunderland wore also featured the logo of club chairman Tom Cowie's company COWIES on the back, and had red sleeves, collars and side panels, but were predominately white. This was the case with the shirts too, which had white sleeves and a v-neck collar - the detail of which was repeated on the cuffs. As well as the sponsor's logo, there was room for three Nike emblems, one on each sleeve and one on the chest, and the club's ship crest. Underneath that were the words 'Milk Cup Final Wembley 1985', also in block capitals.

Goalkeeper Chris Turner had a green top that, whilst including the sponsors logo, did not feature the badge, this despite Nike having issued such kits at the start of the season. Turner regularly wore a top without the badge during the campaign, although there was no need for the tracksuit bottoms he had donned at Watford in round five, and he instead had the same black shorts with red and white trim and red socks with small white detailing as the outfield players. As had been the case before the 1973 FA Cup final, there were issues about the boots the players were asked to wear.

Not for the last time, Sunderland fans left the national stadium downhearted. They still behaved in exemplary fashion however, and it should be a source of pride that the camaraderie shown between the two sets of supporters prompted a car dealership to initiate the Friendship Trophy that is still played for whenever the clubs meet.

THE MATCH

Eighteen-year-old David Corner was making only his fifth first-team appearance. A minute into the second half, he tried to see the ball out for a goal-kick only to be robbed. Consequently Asa Hartford, who had been sent off against Sunderland in the FA Youth Cup final playing for WBA in 1969, saw his shot clip Gordon Chisholm and go in. As with Tony Norman in 1990, a deflection was the only way Sunderland's keeper Chris Turner would be beaten.

Just three minutes after the Canaries went ahead, Sunderland had a chance to equalise from the penalty spot. Dennis van Wijk was penalised for handball by referee Neil Midgley (who would also referee the 1992 FA Cup semi-final between Sunderland and Norwich) as the Dutch defender sought to thwart stand-in skipper Barry Venison. Spot-kick taker Clive Walker hit the post, the chance went begging, after which the game petered out. It was a scrappy encounter - perhaps in keeping with a final where both sides went on to be relegated.

1985

MILK CUP FINAL
SUNDERLAND 0-1 NORWICH CITY
WEMBLEY · SUNDAY 24 MARCH 1985

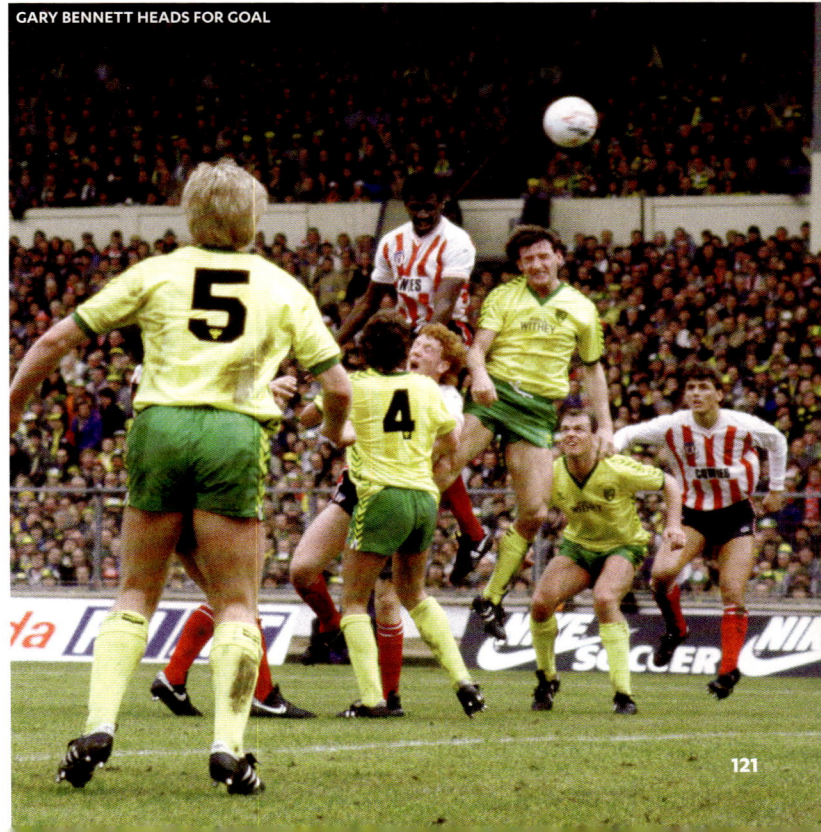

GARY BENNETT HEADS FOR GOAL

1988

MERCANTILE CREDIT FOOTBALL FESTIVAL

SUNDERLAND 0-0 WIGAN ATHLETIC
SUNDERLAND LOST 2-1 ON PENALTIES

WEMBLEY · SATURDAY 16 APRIL 1988

MARCO GABBIADINI

Sunderland made an unusual and ultimately brief Wembley appearance in 1988 as part of the celebrations for 100 years of the Football League and they did so in one of their least remembered kits.

Sixteen teams qualified for the two-day knock-out tournament, based on league results gained between November and March. Sunderland and Wigan represented the third division, while there were two clubs from Division Four, four from Division Two and eight from Division One. During the 15-game qualification period, Sunderland won ten and drew the other five to qualify for a tournament won by Nottingham Forest.

Games on day one where all 16 teams played were 20 minutes each way, with games on day two increasing to 60 minutes. Sunderland did not make it to the second day after being eliminated, and with the competition failing to pique public interest, the kit worn by the Lads remains something of an enigma.

Coverage of the event was minimal, and some supporters have forgotten about Sunderland's fourth trip to Wembley, let alone ever registered that it was the first time they had made the journey and not worn red and white. This despite having already done so at Wigan's Springfield Park in the league a month earlier. Then, the Lads had worn their home shirts, but switched to white shorts, although on a day remembered fondly for their supporters' mud-sliding antics, those shorts did not stay white for long.

With the Mercantile Credit competition rules printed in the festival's official programme stating that "when the colours of two clubs are alike or similar, the team drawn second in each match shall be required to change to a strip which does not include any of the basic colours of the first drawn club" neither Sunderland's traditional kit nor their first choice blue change kit were suitable in light of the Latics' white and blue design.

Sunderland, drawn as the 'away' side, instead wore yellow shirts and shorts with white socks, which was presumably not an issue given that Wigan's socks were blue. French manufacturer Patrick were Sunderland's kit supplier at this point, and they provided shirts featuring shadow stripes with the club badge in the middle of the chest above the black lettering of club sponsor Vaux. Whilst it featured a v-neck collar like the standard kits did, the shorts and socks were much more basic.

THE MATCH

Sunderland failed to have a shot on target and then only scored one of their two penalties in an instant sudden death shoot-out. With goalkeeper Iain Hesford suspended, Tim Carter debuted at Wembley and did well, but was beaten from the spot by Stan McEwan and future Wigan manager Paul Cook.

Writing in The Journal, Jeff Brown said of Sunderland, "The Third Division leaders, as pale and washed out as their insipid all yellow strip, simply never chugged out of first gear." John MacPhail had scored from the spot at Wembley the previous season for Bristol City in a Freight-Rover Trophy final shoot-out and he converted Sunderland's first spot-kick only for Colin Pascoe's penalty to be saved by Northern Ireland international Phil Hughes to give Sunderland their first bitter taste of too many Wembley shoot-out disappointments.

Denis Smith's Red and White Army were actually the boys in blue on the day of their showdown with Swindon Town, and after a disappointing performance on the pitch, had to wait until the 13th of June before their elevation was confirmed as a consequence of Swindon being found guilty of breaching League rules.

The kits from this season are fondly remembered despite the fact the replicas were notoriously susceptible to bobbling and clicks. The team wore traditional home colours in the main, but had a blue away kit and a hugely popular gold third kit that all shared several similarities and when put together were a very attractive set, all featuring rounded wrap over collars and patterned micro-detailing.

By the following season, the gold ones had been tweaked slightly and instead of still having traditional T-shirt sleeves, switched to raglans (which extend up to the collar), a new v-neck and a change from blue to black sponsors logo.

All of the tops had colour coordinated chevron braids down the sleeves, as did the sides of most of the shorts, which in this era were still worn very tight. The only ones not to have these were the plain gold shorts sometimes worn with the third kit, with the first choice for this design being blue.

The away kit also had alternative shorts, yet white was the preference. Sunderland's away record during the regular season was excellent and this was the combination that was used when that form was carried into the Play Off semi-final second leg at Newcastle United.

That evening the Lads showed both immense grit and flair, but that just made Sunderland's off colour showing in the final even more hard to fathom, the side once again wearing their blue away top, but switching the shorts for the blue back up - it should be noted however, that these were not the same as the third kit version and that the braiding was different.

Promotion was announced the same day Sunderland opened a new club shop in Jacky White's Market. It was standing room only in there and supporters may recall how small the store was - tighter even than the shorts it initially stocked.

THE MATCH

This was the first season where the Play-Off finals were staged at Wembley. In energy-sapping conditions, the G-Force front two of Eric Gates and Marco Gabbiadini seemed to have to expend most of their energy working to stop Ossie Ardiles' talented Robins team from playing out from the back.

Steve White and Tom Jones in particular brought good saves out of Tony Norman who looked in unbeatable form only to be undone by a 25th minute shot from Alan McLoughlin that he had comfortably covered, until it took a deflection off skipper Gary Bennett and left him with no chance.

1990

BARCLAYS LEAGUE DIVISION TWO PLAY-OFF FINAL

SUNDERLAND 0-1 SWINDON TOWN

WEMBLEY · MONDAY 28 MAY 1990

GARY OWERS HOLDS OFF SWINDON'S STEVE FOLEY

1992

FA CUP FINAL
SUNDERLAND 0-2 LIVERPOOL
WEMBLEY · SATURDAY 9 MAY 1992

ANTON ROGAN, RAY HOUGHTON & GARY BENNETT

The hugely popular away kit worn against Liverpool is synonymous with many people's memories of the era, despite the final being the only game in the run in which it was seen. Before that, Sunderland had mainly used their traditional colours, although at Oxford United and Chelsea they did make use of their alternative red shorts.

Both kits had been introduced at the start of the season with the shorts using the same design each time, but in different colours, and as well as the second version to go with the home top, there was a back-up white choice if needed for the away kit. The socks were also the same design and now featured the club's crest, which had been tweaked slightly to show a black background behind a white ship. The shorts and socks both featured the manufacturer Hummel's two chevron pattern and this was repeated on the shirts, although these were otherwise quite different from one another - the straightforward home shirt featuring a polo collar and the away kit incorporating a blue, white, black and green shoulder and sleeve pattern to go with the white body and wrap-over collar.

Unlike Bob Stokoe in 1973, manager Malcolm Crosby, in only his third game as permanent manager, wore a suit for the final, although the players again had cracking pre-match gear, shellsuits now as opposed to tracksuits, which like the shirts had FA Cup Final Wembley 1992 embroidered around the badges. Shellsuits were huge during the early part of the decade, but whilst not every fashion craze passes the test of time, the kit used here remains a perennial favourite with fans.

THE MATCH

Having finished 19th in Division Two, Sunderland were the lowest placed cup-finalists since Leicester City in 1949, when they had also been 19th in the second division. Just as Leicester lost by two goals to the team who had finished sixth in the top tier, so did Sunderland. Whereas Leicester lost to Wolves, the Lads succumbed to Liverpool.

At 0-0, captain Paul Bracewell saw a goal-bound effort deflected, but the big moment saw John Byrne miss a great opportunity that would have put Sunderland ahead and made him only the tenth player ever to have scored in every round.

Level at the break, Malcolm Crosby's men ran out of steam in the second half as a young Steve McManaman proved too hot to handle. Two minutes into the second half, Michael Thomas atoned for the goal he scored for Arsenal to deny Liverpool the league title three years earlier, as he spectacularly put them ahead. Sunderland were still in contention, but after Tony Norman was beaten by his international teammate Ian Rush in the 68th minute, the game was up. For Rush, it was a record-breaking fifth final goal.

Sunderland's players actually received winners' medals by accident, but only had them for a few minutes before handing them to the deserved victors who also had a brand new trophy to display. The cup itself - made by Birmingham company Toye, Kenning & Spencer - was the fourth in the history of the world's oldest football competition, but would only be contested for until 2014 until it was replaced again.

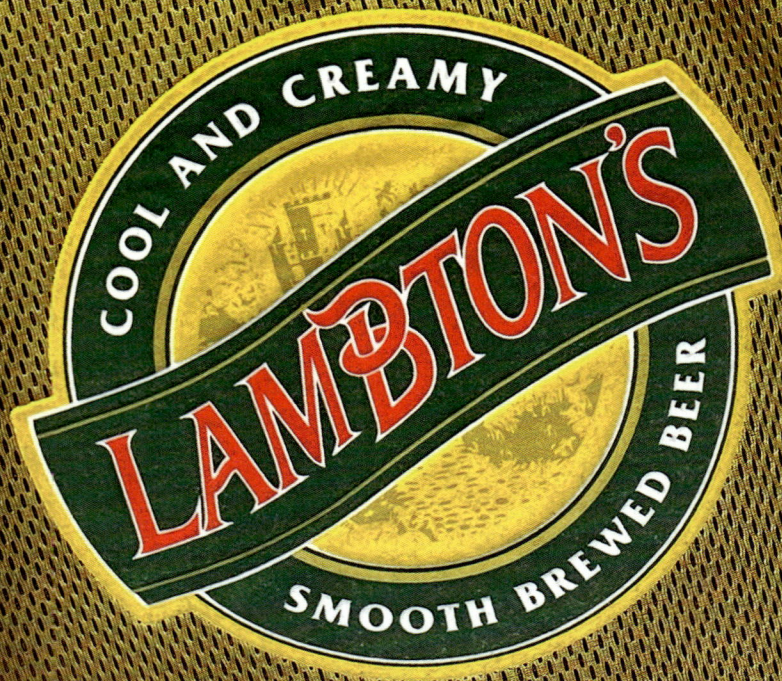

During previous Wembley visits, Sunderland's goalkeepers would usually wear the same shorts and socks as the outfield players, but this time, Lionel Perez had dedicated white socks and blue shorts that matched his shirt, which like the outfield players featured the club crest in the middle of the chest, but did not include an additional one on the back below the collar as the outfield ones.

The Lads had visited Charlton two months before and worn their gold away kit with the alternative navy blue shorts, and gold socks with navy blue turnovers. Although Charlton then replaced their home kit for the final, Sunderland used the same strip, but included a patch that read 'Div 1 Play Offs Wembley 25-5-98'.

This was Sunderland's second stab at the gold run. On the final day of the standard season the Lads won at Swindon Town whilst wearing their away strip, but were condemned to the Play-Offs due to results elsewhere.

The shirts were quite heavy to wear and when wet, seemed as if they could feel like chainmail. It had been a long and hard season and playing such a pulsating final under the beating sun and on an energy-sapping pitch made for an extremely draining day, not least for Michael Gray.

The players reportedly drowned their sorrows on the return home, but during the journey the foundations for the following season were already being laid. Yet another Wembley defeat was an undoubted blow, but by August a galvanised Sunderland would start hitting back.

THE MATCH

Probably only Sunderland could score ten times at Wembley and still lose. Four goals and six successful spot-kicks out of six were not enough as Sunderland-raised Clive Mendonca scored a hat-trick and converted the first penalty of the shoot-out as Charlton went on to win.

Remarkably for such a goal-fest, there was only one goal in the first half, Mendonca giving the London side the lead mid-way through the half. Sunderland turned the tables early in the second period, Niall Quinn equalising five minutes after the re-start. Eight minutes later, SuperKev put the Lads ahead with his 35th goal of the campaign to break Brian Clough's post-war seasonal scoring record. The goal was Sunderland's 100th of the season in all competitions. Mendonca equalised with 19 minutes remaining, but within two minutes Quinn restored the advantage, making it 3-2 before Richard Rufus (who had debuted at Sunderland in 1994) headed his first ever goal to tie the game at three-all in the 85th minute.

Nine minutes into extra-time, Nicky Summerbee shot Sunderland into the lead for the third time. The lead lasted just four minutes before that man Mendonca laid claim to the match ball as he made it four-all.

Summerbee, Allan Johnston, Kevin Ball, Chris Makin, Alex Rae and Niall Quinn all held their nerve to score in the shoot-out, but it was left to Gray to be the fall guy as Sasa Ilic saved his weary and no doubt nerve-riddled shot. Sunderland and Gray - who would be capped by England the following season - came back stronger, but this was a tough one to take.

1998

NATIONWIDE DIVISION ONE PLAY-OFF FINAL

SUNDERLAND 4-4 CHARLTON ATHLETIC
A.E.T. · SUNDERLAND LOST 7-6 ON PENALTIES

WEMBLEY · MONDAY 25 MAY 1998

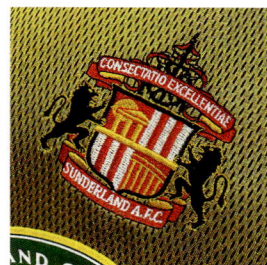

SUPERKEV ON TARGET FOR GOAL NUMBER TWO

CAPITAL ONE CUP FINAL

SUNDERLAND 1-3 MANCHESTER CITY

WEMBLEY · SUNDAY 2 MARCH 2014

A JUBILANT FABIO BORINI

This was the second time Sunderland had reached the League Cup final, and it was the first occasion since the earlier appearance in the same competition that they wore their traditional colours at Wembley, with the Lads using their adidas home strip featuring the maker's logo in the middle of the chest.

The shirt had a white base and like most of Sunderland's kits in the early years with the firm, their three stripe motif ended at the bicep to make room for sleeve patches.

The three stripes were repeated on black shorts and black socks which had red trim, although alternative socks with the colours reversed were available for other games. The patterns were also used for the goalkeeper kit, with Vito Mannone, who turned 26 on the day of the game, wearing a green strip that had black on the sleeves and mesh panels on the shoulders. Mannone finished the campaign being named Player of the Season just as fellow stopper Chris Turner had done in 1985 when the club last reached the final.

Sunderland fans dared to dream as their side walked out at Wembley wearing drill tops from that season's training range and these, like the shirts, proudly displayed the text 'Capital One Cup Final Manchester City FC v Sunderland AFC Wembley Stadium 2nd March 2014'. It was a date that nearly went down as one of the club's greatest.

THE MATCH

Under Gus Poyet, Sunderland's philosophy was to play possession football with Lee Cattermole the conduit which so much of their play flowed through. Sunderland led at half time and indeed led for longer in the game than City did. Only ten minutes had gone when Fabio Borini tucked the ball beyond future Sunderland keeper Costel Pantilimon. Before half time, the Italian striker looked as if he might double the lead, only to be denied by a terrific tackle from City skipper Vincent Kompany.

Ten minutes into the second half Sunderland still led, but the game spun on two goals in as many minutes. The equaliser came from Yaya Toure, a former Champions League winner with Barcelona (when he played in the 2009 final against Sunderland's 2014 captain John O'Shea). Toure hit a speculative 25-yarder that curled into the top corner. It was a great goal, but perhaps one that even Toure could pull off only once out of 100 attempts.

Before anyone could grumble that if the footballing Gods had smiled on Sunderland the shot would have cleared the bar, Manchester City were ahead. French international Samir Nasri scored another goal right out of the top drawer. City were leading, but they had been forced to produce their best in order to be there.

Sunderland went on to lose 3-1, but the scoreline was harsh, the third goal from Jesus Navas coming from a lightning-fast last-minute break, just after Steven Fletcher had fluffed a chance to equalise.

En route to the Football League Trophy final nine players got to wear a Sunderland kit for the first time, with five prospects debuting in the group stages during a win at Morecambe.

In that match, the Lads reused the previous season's blue away kit. The strip had been reintroduced earlier in the campaign against Bradford City, and with the Shrimpers' wearing red and black, Sunderland's regular choices were again unsuitable. The only other time Sunderland travelled in the competition prior to the final was when they visited Bristol Rovers in the semi-final, and for this they wore their standard red and white shirts with black shorts.

It was the same combination as had been used in the league fixture at the Memorial Stadium ten days earlier. Both games finished 2-0 and proved to be the only occasions Sunderland won an away game this season with this pairing - all other victories in red and white on the road came when the alternative red shorts were being used.

The home kit's stripes looked more traditional than on the design they replaced, and with Climalite materials being used again, the reds were micro ribbed and the whites were perforated. The socks meanwhile, reverted to red having been black the season before.

For the final, the club re-released shirts and training wear with the same block capital lettering reading 'Checkatrade Trophy Final Portsmouth FC v Sunderland AFC Wembley Stadium 31st March 2019' that was added to those of the players.

Their strips were further supplemented with the logo of Sunderland's first ever back of short sponsor, Eleven Sports Media, who came on board in time for the final and also began providing fan engagement technology and services to the club. On the toss of a coin, Pompey wore blue socks rather than their normal red to avoid duplicating Sunderland's.

THE MATCH

The crowd of over 85,000 was a record for the competition and higher than for Sunderland's previous five trips to the national stadium. It was also over 3,000 more than saw the same season's League Cup final between Chelsea and Manchester City.

Aiden McGeady gave Sunderland the lead with a superb 38th minute free kick. As in their previous Wembley appearance, the lead lasted for about half of the 90 minutes before the Lads were pegged back. On this occasion, a header from Nathan Thompson took the match into extra-time which as is so often the case at Wembley, was a cagey affair contested by tired players.

Six minutes from the end, Pompey winger Jamal Lowe produced a moment of real quality to lob goalkeeper Jon McLaughlin and make it 2-1. This time it was Sunderland's turn to leave it late to score, as with barely a minute to go McGeady levelled.

McGeady, Lynden Gooch, Max Power and Luke O'Nien converted with Lee Cattermole the unlucky man to have his shot saved. Like Michael Gray in 1998, 'Catts' was at least commended on having the bottle to step forward.

2019 |||

CHECKATRADE TROPHY FINAL
SUNDERLAND 2-2 PORTSMOUTH
A.E.T. · SUNDERLAND LOST 5-4 ON PENALTIES
WEMBLEY · SUNDAY 31 MARCH 2019

AIDEN McGEADY'S LATE LEVELLER

2019

SKY BET LEAGUE ONE PLAY-OFF FINAL

SUNDERLAND 1-2 CHARLTON ATHLETIC

WEMBLEY · SUNDAY 26 MAY 2019

LEWIS MORGAN

As the 'away' side, Sunderland were required to wear their black change kit and having used their home version against Portsmouth in the recent Football League Trophy final, it meant the club were still to wear the same strip more than once at Wembley.

Had they been able to wear their traditional colours, Sunderland might have still been showcasing a different look anyway as in the build-up to the game, the club released its new 2019-20 design.

It wasn't seen as an issue though, the side had only lost once in the kit prior to the final and when it was released, it was well received despite there being a black third kit the season before. Whilst the shades were similar, and the badges were still on shields, there were enough design differences; the kit now being less matt like in appearance and adidas' three stripes moving from the sides of the shirt to the shoulders.

A smart red trim was used that matched the logo of Betdaq, who were also Charlton's kit sponsor, and whose deal with Sunderland had been brokered by future non-executive director Tom Sloanes. In white, were the logos of the club's other partners Utilita and Eleven Sports Media and the shirts were adorned with match details reading 'Sky Bet League One Play-Off Final Charlton Athletic FC v Sunderland AFC Wembley Stadium 26th May 2019'.

This was even longer than the text featured on the shirts for the Checkatrade Trophy final, although this time, it was not all in upper case font and unlike that match, the Lads did not have any additional walk-on gear - against Portsmouth the side had entered the fray and sang the national anthem whilst wearing training tops.

Anybody looking a bit closer at the kits might have noticed that the micro shadow detailing of the shirts was a smaller scale version of the pattern on front of the goalkeepers tops that season. Playing in both Wembley visits, John McLaughlin wore the aqua option for this match having been in maroon and black during the first game.

THE MATCH

Charlton defender Naby Sarr's own-goal gave Sunderland an early lead, but just four minutes later Max Power had to limp out of the action, having been fouled earlier by Sarr who was later cautioned for a foul on captain George Honeyman.

Power was replaced by on-loan Celtic winger Lewis Morgan, but the former Celtic winger Sunderland really needed was still on the bench. Having scored twice in the recent visit to Wembley, Aiden McGeady was only fit enough to come on for the latter stages. He was introduced with 18 minutes to play as Sunderland strove for a winner. Charlton had equalised ten minutes before half time through on-loan Rotherham-man Ben Purrington.

Just as the match looked like going to extra-time, German defender Patrick Bauer got on the end of a free-kick and reacted quickest to score at the second attempt from close range, after Tom Flanagan blocked his first effort. There were six seconds to go and barely time to kick-off.

Sunderland won the English Football League Trophy for the first time, but ending a rotten Wembley run that had stretched back to 1985 was just as gratifying.

With many supporters struggling with Coronavirus restrictions it was nice to have something positive to focus on, and in the build-up, competition sponsors Papa John's temporarily renamed their Fulwell branch 'Papa Lee's' after head coach Lee Johnson.

During their run to the final two years earlier, Sunderland's first ever club specific sleeve sponsor had been a rival brand, with a Durham based franchise of Domino's putting their logo on the shirts in the semi-final. Now wearing their Nike home kit for this season's final, Sunderland again had a one-off sleeve sponsor, with the logo of asbestos specialists and long-term club partner UKasl being one of several additions.

Including an open 'placket' collar and red central stripe, the back of the shirts were also striped whilst on the inside was the insignia 'Ha'way the Lads'. As well as the standard club crest and manufacturer's logo, the kits featured regular first-team back of shirt and shorts sponsors Utilita and Eleven Sports Media, an NHS motif, competition sponsor logos, Mind charity player name and numbering font and EFL 'Not Today or Any Day' campaign patches.

Players also wore black arm bands in honour of a Tranmere fan that had recently passed away, and for good measure both the outfield shirts and Lee Burge's orange goalkeeping shirt bore the words 'Sunderland AFC v Tranmere Rovers FC Papa John's Trophy Final 14th March 2021 Wembley Stadium'.

There were no walk on tops, although Sunderland did release a hugely popular range of deep red training gear that was used during the warm-ups. At this point the omens were looking good - Sunderland's previous Wembley successes had come against teams in white, and the match was played on the 73rd day of the year. Just like in 1973, a 1-0 win was about to transpire.

THE MATCH

After eight consecutive unsuccessful trips to Wembley, Sunderland finally won on an occasion when due to Covid 19, no supporters were allowed to attend. They were there in spirit, as evidenced by the phenomenal raising of £165,000 for four local charities thanks to a virtual ticket campaign that was the brainchild of supporter Peter Richardson.

Both Sunderland and Tranmere were in good form going into the final which was a tight affair settled by one goal, but what a good goal it was. The mercurial Aiden McGeady's link-ups with centre-forward Charlie Wyke had been the story of the season, but on this occasion the Irish international threaded a through ball to USA cap Lynden Gooch who stormed forward and provided an emphatic finish.

Conor McLaughlin went close to doubling the lead late on only for his header to be tipped onto the bar by Rovers keeper Scott Davies, but as in 1973 a scoreline of 1-0 was sufficient to bring silverware to Sunderland.

2021

PAPA JOHN'S TROPHY FINAL

SUNDERLAND 1-0 TRANMERE ROVERS

WEMBLEY · SUNDAY 14 MARCH 2021

MAX POWER AND THE LADS WITH THE TROPHY

RARE CAT SIGHTINGS

The advent of floodlighting during the 1950s had a major impact on football and proved to be a hit across the country. Not only did fans relish being able to see games in the evening, but at Sunderland, with the club staging several prestigious friendlies following the installation of floodlights at Roker Park, they also got to witness the Lads take to the pitch wearing specially produced kits, with the shirts made from a shiny red material designed to be easier to pick out.

It would be extremely rare now to see Sunderland playing on home soil in anything but red and white striped shirts with black shorts, but there have been several other instances of this over the years, and if that is hard for some younger supporters to comprehend, they will struggle even more to believe that in the same decade, the side even wore black and white stripes in some FA Cup ties.

Drawn at home to Southampton in 1951, when in that competition it was still a requirement for either just the home side or otherwise both sides to change strips if there was a clash, Sunderland had to borrow a set of strips from Newcastle United. The switch did not prove to be an issue as the Black (and white) Cats won 2-0, but then again, there is one theory that Sunderland's initial move to red and white was after the acquisition of such kits from another north-eastern rival, Teesside-based South Bank, so perhaps it was not that unusual after all.

In 1955 and 1956, Sunderland reached consecutive FA Cup semi-finals, the second time coming after being taken to a replay by Sheffield United in round five. With the Blades borrowing a blue and white change kit from

NEWCASTLE V SUNDERLAND 1956 FA CUP 6TH ROUND

BILL HOLDEN – SCORER OF BOTH GOALS IN THE 1956 FA CUP WIN OVER NEWCASTLE

THE LADS IN BLACK AND WHITE STRIPES V SOUTHAMPTON IN 1951

neighbours Barnsley, Sunderland again turned out in black and white during both games, the second of which saw a narrow Roker Park victory to set up a clash, ironically, with cup holders and kit lenders Newcastle.

There have been few derbies between the two clubs as high profile as this, with over 60,000 spectators witnessing Sunderland win a game for which they wore Arsenal-style red shirts with white sleeves against their white shirted hosts.

The cup run ended at Hillsborough, with Sunderland, now able to wear their traditional colours once more, being beaten by Birmingham City. Perhaps then, the unfamiliar strips had been lucky, although during the 1963-64 campaign, Sunderland were a strong side and on their way to promotion without having to rely on good fortune or chance. They were so strong in fact that in a friendly at Roker they beat a Benfica side that just six months earlier reached a European Cup Final and had won the competition in the two seasons before that.

On that evening, Sunderland wore an all white strip similar to that of Leeds United, the side whom Sunderland went up with at the end of the season. When the two teams met in the FA Cup three years later, the tie had to be settled via a second replay, but during the first match on Wearside, the Lads were dressed in their all red change kit.

1971 saw a further instance of Sunderland playing at home in unusual fashion when Orient came to town for another FA Cup match. With the Lads wearing all sky blue, but losing 3-0, the North Sea air had probably turned blue as well come full time. Sunderland had worn that colour a few times previously, but two years later came an even lesser-seen kit, a red shirt with large white collars and sections down the sides that was used for a draw away at West Bromwich Albion.

In 1979, supporters got two Sunderland kits for the price of one when Queens Park Rangers travelled north. With one of their change kits at this point a red and white halved shirt like some of the designs worn by Sunderland in their early days, QPR mimicked the Lads even more by having to borrow the blue shirt and white shorts change kit of their hosts.

This presumably didn't confuse the Lads too much, who still won comfortably despite the possible temptation to pass the ball to the opposition by mistake.

BILLY HUGHES AT WEST BROMWICH ALBION DURING THE 1973-74 SEASON

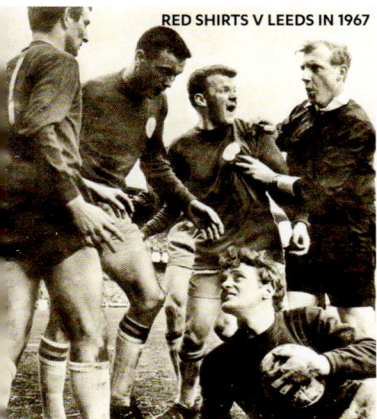
RED SHIRTS V LEEDS IN 1967

QPR IN SAFC KIT AT ROKER PARK IN 1979

In goal for the visitors was Chris Woods, who perhaps got a taste for wearing Sunderland gear - 18 years later he played for the club during the final game at Roker Park.

The change strip Sunderland had loaned out was still in use in 1981, but was not deemed suitable for a fresh trip to The Hawthorns. At this point, SAFC were interchanging use of the shirt with the white version of a very similar template. The white one had even been seen in a now increasingly rare example of the Lads playing at Roker in something other than red and white stripes during a friendly against Coventry City, prior to the start of the season, but this too would have clashed with West Brom's kit and so Umbro produced an all red shirt that was worn with black shorts and red socks.

THE ONE-OFF RED SHIRT SUNDERLAND WORE AT WEST BROMWICH ALBION DURING THE 1980-81 SEASON

LE COQ SPORTIF'S RED DESIGN WORN 1981-83

TUBORG

THE ONE-OFF ORANGE SHIRT SUNDERLAND WORE AT HUDDERSFIELD ON THE OPENING DAY OF THE 1986-87 SEASON

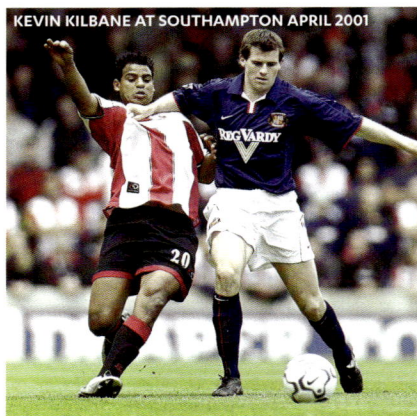

KEVIN KILBANE AT SOUTHAMPTON APRIL 2001

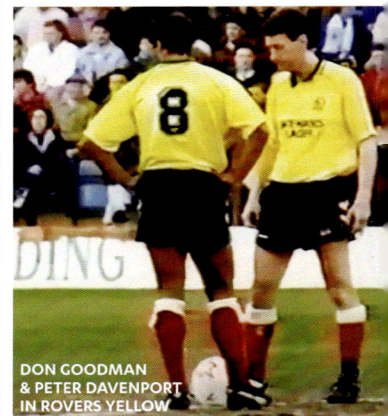

DON GOODMAN & PETER DAVENPORT IN ROVERS YELLOW

When photographs of a long sleeved version emerged online in 2020, some supporters initially mistook it for a goalkeeper kit that was sometimes used by Barry Siddall in the same era. There was a royal blue version of the goalkeepers top also, but on closer inspection, the collar design of the outfield shirt had changed, and it was made with a different material.

After the West Brom game, Sunderland only had two more competitive games before they changed kit manufacturer, and it was a case of going from that little remembered red shirt to one many fans would love to be able to forget. Le Coq Sportif's infamous design for the home strip was panned by many, but the accompanying third strip, which was red with white pinstripes and trim, was still only used for a small handful of matches.

At least Baggies fans were getting to see these rare kits in person - one of the few outings was back at West Bromwich a year and four days after the appearance of the red Umbro shirts, although this time, it was the Sunderland supporters that left happiest after seeing their side avenge the previous season's defeat with an important 3-2 victory.

Seen even less than that third kit, was a strip worn by Sunderland for the opening game of the fateful 1986-87 season, which ended with a dismal relegation to the third tier despite starting brightly, or brightly orange to be exact. This was the first time Sunderland wore kit supplied by manufacturer Patrick, with the Orange Kit Cats beating Huddersfield Town 2-0 with two goals scored after taking a half-time break.

Based on the same template as the blue change kit that was used thereafter, the Tuborg sponsor logo was in a black font, but this is one of the few features that can be determined from match action photographs alone as they are all believed to be in black and white.

Instead, the authors are grateful to a supporter who was able to provide photographs of the shirt from his private collection, one of which is shown on this page. When Sunderland had cause for a third kit again in the following season, Patrick instead provided a yellow one that in addition to being used for the Mercantile Credit Football Festival had an outing at Preston North End in the league two months earlier.

Sunderland could have perhaps done with a set of spare kits during April 1992, when the club had to play ten games and the kitman was presumably

140

working around the clock. He at least got a bit of respite following the trip to Blackburn Rovers, for which the referee insisted Sunderland needed to borrow Blackburn's yellow away shirts to go with their traditional shorts and socks.

Earlier in the month though, when Charlton Athletic arrived at Roker with a dark blue and black change kit, it was Sunderland that were required to switch to the alternative red shorts that were seen regularly on the road during this period.

A year and one day after the visit of the Addicks, the shorts were back out on show for the trip to Grimsby Town, where Sunderland were again forced into an unfamiliar combination. Grimsby, who like Blackburn had been a season earlier, were supplied by Ribero and lent Terry Butcher's men their blotchy salmon coloured third shirt for the game, although Mick Harford was soon seeing more red after being sent off.

The Lads eventually fell to a narrow defeat, but it was hardly a case of men against boys, despite the side looking like school children that had forgotten their PE kit and been forced to delve into the lost property box.

These ad hoc changes were what possibly led to the club introducing a new third kit two months into the 1993-94 season. A yellow strip with black shoulders and detailing, it was worn on several occasions and was very popular with supporters, but is now considered rare as it was the last regularly used strip not to be made available for retail by the club. The player issues are therefore prized items for collectors and are invariably snapped up quickly when they become available.

THE YELLOW & BLACK THIRD KIT FROM 1993-94

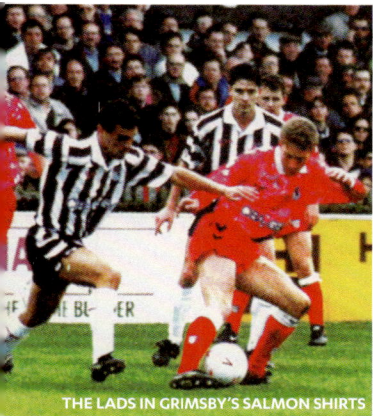

THE LADS IN GRIMSBY'S SALMON SHIRTS

LEE CATTERMOLE AT PALACE IN 2014

Formalisation of the rules and the prevalence of third kits since the creation of the Premier League mean colour clashes are few and far between, although victories whilst wearing one-off kits against Southampton in 2001, when a navy blue shirt was used, and Crystal Palace in 2014, when the white kit referred to by Lee Cattermole in the foreword of this book was used, might lead to some Black Cat supporters wishing for more.

For the kit enthusiasts amongst the fan base however, just the rare kits themselves are an intriguing element of Sunderland's colourful history.

THE ONE-OFF WHITE SHIRT WORN IN 2014

SAFC BLACK CAT'ALOGUE

HOME AND AWAY KITS
FROM THE STADIUM OF LIGHT ERA

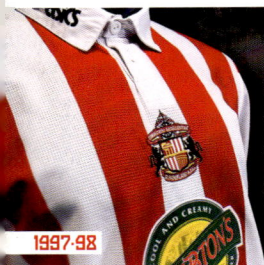

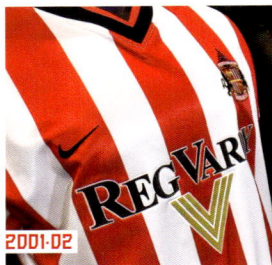

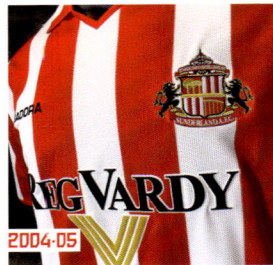

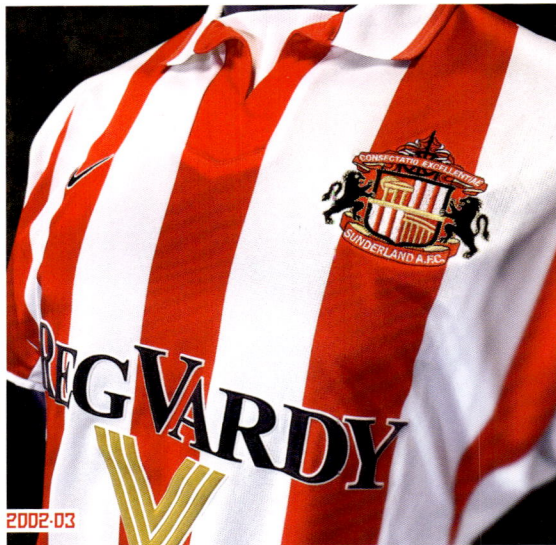

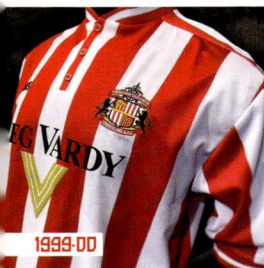

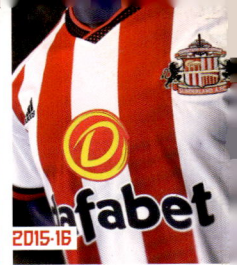

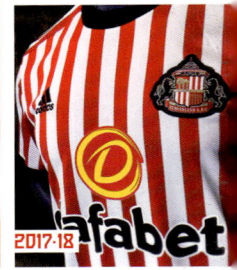

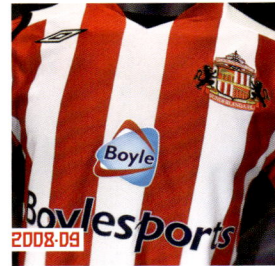

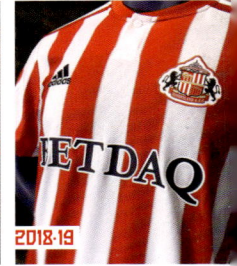

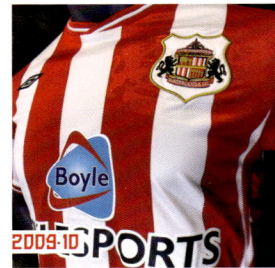

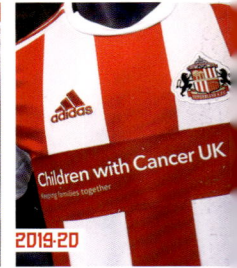

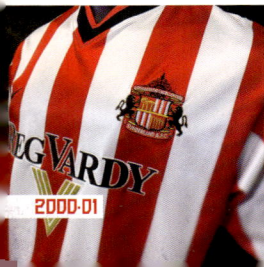

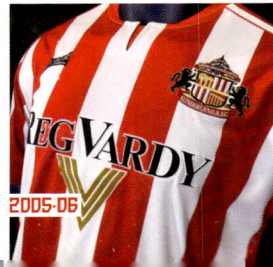

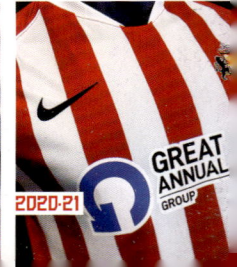

2006-07

2011-12

2015-16

2016-17

2007-08

2017-18

1997-98

2001-02

2004-05

1998-99

2008-09

2012-13

2018-19

1999-00

2002-03

2009-10

2013-14

2019-20

2000-01

2003-04

2005-06

2010-11

2014-15

2020-21

CONSECTATIO EXCELLENTIAE

SUNDERLAND A.F.C.

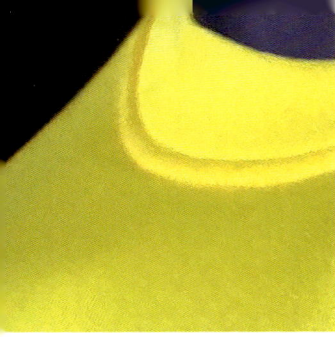

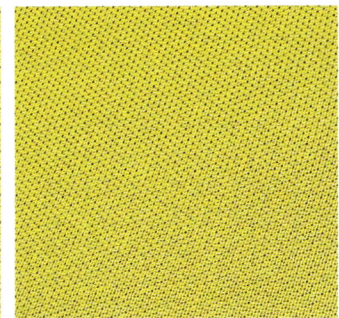

HA'WAY
THE LADS

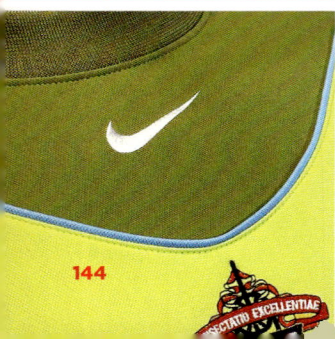